RECOGNIZING FOREIGN GOVERNMENTS

RECOGNIZING FOREIGN GOVERNMENTS

THE PRACTICE OF THE UNITED STATES

L. THOMAS GALLOWAY
WITH A FOREWORD BY R.R. BAXTER

American Enterprise Institute for Public Policy Research
Washington, D.C.

L. Thomas Galloway is a public interest lawyer at the Center for Law and Social Policy in Washington, D.C.

Library of Congress Cataloging in Publication Data

Galloway, L. Thomas.
    Recognizing foreign governments.

    (AEI studies ; 180)
    Bibliography: p.
    1. Recognition (International law)   2. United
States—Foreign relations.   I. Title.   II. Series:
American Enterprise Institute for Public Policy
Research.   AEI studies ; 180.
JX4044.G33   341.26   77-28468
ISBN 0-8447-3280-X

AEI studies 180

ISBN 0-8447-3280-X

Printed in the United States of America

CONTENTS

FOREWORD

This book brings to light a quiet change in the American perspective on the recognition of states and governments—a change that has taken place almost imperceptibly and without an antecedent statement that there was to be a change in policy. What has happened in recent years is that the U.S. government has attempted to avoid defining its relations with newly established governments in terms of recognition or nonrecognition. Prior to this change, the institution of recognition, far from helping to solve problems, had itself become part of the problem.

The treatises and the casebooks have continued to treat the recognition of governments in particular as if it were a living institution. However, not only in the United States but in other countries as well, recognition has materially diminished in importance as a concept of international law and of diplomacy.

In the practice of the United States, the change has come on a case-by-case basis, the handling of one case forming a helpful precedent for the resolution of the next. This gradual change, which has not been based on any declared policy, has reflected what might be described as a common-law approach to the problem frequently faced in the U.S. Department of State. Only after Mr. Galloway's book had been completed did Deputy Secretary of State Warren Christopher, in a speech on normalization of diplomatic relations delivered at Occidental College,[1] lay out some of the considerations that guide U.S. policy. "The premise of our present policy," he said, "is that diplomatic relations do not constitute a seal of approval." He described the consequences that follow from that premise:

---

[1] Department of State, Bureau of Public Affairs, Office of Media Services, Speech on "Nationalization of Diplomatic Relations," June 11, 1977.

The reality is that, in this day and age, coups and other unscheduled changes of government are not exceptional developments. Withholding diplomatic relations from these regimes, after they have obtained effective control, penalizes us. It means that we forsake much of the chance to influence the attitudes and conduct of a new regime. Without relations, we forfeit opportunities to transmit our values and communicate our policies. Isolation may well bring out the worst in the new government.

For the same reasons, we eschew withdrawal of diplomatic relations except in rare instances—for example, the outbreak of war or events which make it physically impossible to maintain a diplomatic presence in another capital.

He went on to describe the efforts made during the administration of President Carter to establish normal diplomatic relations with other countries, including Vietnam, the People's Republic of China, Cuba, and the Congo Republic.

It is reasonable to suppose that the present policy has been influenced by the fact that various forms of diplomatic relations, if not the totality of normal relations, have been carried on with political entities or governments that the United States did not recognize. The existence of what is in fact a separate state or government cannot be completely ignored; the realities of international life often call for dealings with such a state or government. The United States negotiated armistices with the North Korean forces and what amounted to a peace settlement with the Democratic Republic of Vietnam and the Provisional Revolutionary Government of Vietnam. Even before normal diplomatic relations were established with the German Diplomatic Republic, the United States had certain dealings with that state. And the presence of a U.S. mission in Peking demonstrates in the most dramatic form the willingness of this country to carry on something close to normal diplomatic relations with a government that it has never recognized.

Recognition and nonrecognition had come to have political and moral connotations under the varying recognition policies followed by successive administrations, as described by Mr. Galloway in this book. If the United States was too slow to recognize a new regime that had been established by a coup d'etat, the new government would regard the conduct of the United States as offensive. If the United States recognized such a new government early in its life, the previously established government would regard that recognition as improper, and indeed unlawful. If recognition became a stamp of approval and an indication of legitimacy, to grant it or to deny it to a government or administration could be looked upon as an impermissible intervention in the domestic affairs of that state. By contrast, the reduction or suspension or resumption of diplomatic relations could be fine-tuned in proportion to the confidence of the U.S. government in the capacity of the "old" and "new" governments to speak for the state. Nonrecognition could entail the withdrawal of U.S. representation in a country where an extraconstitutional change of government was taking place, but it was at the very stage of changing administrations that it was most important that the United States should have the means of reporting what was happening and of dealing with those in effective control of the state.

Thus, whether recognition should be granted or withdrawn has become a nonproblem. If anyone should venture to ask the Department of State about the recognition policy of the U.S. government in a particular instance, he is usually informed that no question of recognition arises. Of course, the question will have to be answered in some cases—for example, in proceedings in U.S. courts involving foreign governments—but such cases cannot be expected to arise frequently.

Mr. Galloway's study of the past practice of the United States and of its contemporary policy in respect to recognition is based upon a close examination of the practice of the Department of State. He takes us behind the scenes to show us what has been happening in the United States and in other countries and articulates what has in fact become the policy of the department. The moral to be learned is that an institution of the law that causes more problems than it solves must be rejected and replaced by working arrangements that are flexible and realistic. The partial withdrawal of law from this area of international relations will facilitate the maintenance of relations with states in which extraconstitutional changes of government are taking place, and that in itself is a good thing. It is much to be hoped that this book will encourage states which cling to the institution of recognition of governments to follow the course set by the United States and by many other countries of the world.

R. R. Baxter
Cambridge, Mass.

PREFACE

The recognition of foreign governments that come to power through extraconstitutional means has played a significant role in the conduct of American foreign policy since the early days of the republic. I became interested in the subject during my sojourn in 1972 as an extern with the Legal Adviser's Office of the Department of State. The more I pursued it, the clearer it became that the executive branch, Congress, and numerous academic figures had never reached agreement on such basic, recurring issues as what recognition is, when it should be accorded to a foreign government, and what it means once granted. The literature, which is profuse, reflects the conflict and confusion that have marked United States recognition practice.

This study attempts to dispel at least some of the confusion by examining the recognition practice of the United States, emphasizing recent experience. The study examines the U.S. response to most successful extraconstitutional changes of government between 1961 and 1976, a period that has yet to receive substantial academic attention.

Numerous difficulties arose in assembling reliable information for this portion of the study, and in determining what constitutes an extraconstitutional change of government. Deciding whether a given change of government is in accord with the domestic law of a state, or whether the change was accomplished through duress or force, is a tricky business. Therefore, I adopted a pragmatic approach, and included in the study all changes of government that caused the United States to consider seriously whether the question of recognition was raised. This approach also provides the broadest view of the development of United States policy.

The historical overview of the recognition practice of the United States from the time of Thomas Jefferson through the beginning of the Kennedy administration in Chapter 1 provides the necessary backdrop to understand recognition practice in more recent times (Chapters 2–4). Chapter 5 centers on the recognition practice of other nations in the world and should be useful both for the information it imparts and for the guide it provides in evaluating United States practice. This part of the study was made possible by a communication sent by the Department of State in 1969 requesting all United States embassies to determine the recognition practice of their host state by consulting with its foreign ministry. I updated this material in 1975 by asking the Washington embassies of these foreign states whether their recognition policy had changed since the Department of State survey in 1969.

The final portion of the study, U.S. recognition practice for the future (Chapter 6), reflects my own views on desirable U.S. policy, and in no way represents the position of the Department of State, either in 1972 or today.

Professor Richard R. Baxter of the Harvard Law School has my warmest thanks for introducing me to a topic that has proven fascinating and intellectually satisfying. John Norton Moore, my professor at the University of Virginia School of Law, who introduced me to the field of international law and who succeeded Professor Baxter as counsellor on international law at the Department of State, also deserves special thanks.

Jeanette Moe is responsible for most of the typing of the many drafts this manuscript has undergone. She worked long and hard with good cheer, offering many valuable suggestions. She did this without pay and while a full-time secretary for the law firm at which I worked for two years. For this she has my deep gratitude and respect.

I also note the help of various lawyers within the Legal Adviser's Office of the Department of State, and of Dr. Ronald Landau, a diplomatic historian in the Historical Office of the department. In the course of his duties Dr. Landau has done extensive work on United States recognition practice toward Latin America. I have drawn upon his excellent work in completing this study, and I acknowledge my debt. I would also like to thank Joan Wadlow, associate dean, College of Arts and Sciences, University of Nebraska, and Professor Charles L. Cochran, United States Naval Academy, for permission to use their data which appear in Appendix B.

Despite an author's best efforts, errors can usually be found in a completed manuscript, and I am sure that this study is no exception. I have checked source material as carefully as possible, and various individuals, both within the Department of State and without, have reviewed the manuscript. My thanks for their time, their suggestions, and their observations. The errors that remain are my own, for which I take responsibility.

L. Thomas Galloway
Washington, D.C.

INTRODUCTION

The recognition of foreign governments is an often-practiced but little understood area of foreign policy. Although the practice of recognizing governments that come to power through extraconstitutional means is over two centuries old and literally thousands of new governments have been recognized, much remains unclear about both the practical and the theoretical side of recognition.

Foreign policy decision makers have utilized recognition in myriad ways, depending on the political circumstances of the time and their perception of the national interest involved in a change of government. Thus, for example, the United States has used recognition as a political tool to support antimonarchical governments (under George Washington), to advance economic imperialism (under Theodore Roosevelt), to promote constitutional government (under Woodrow Wilson), and to halt the spread of communism (under Dwight Eisenhower). The practice of other states is similarly diverse.

While the use of the recognition instrument in order to achieve political objectives may be justifiable, the instrument is often employed without the development of an adequate analytical framework to explain it. Consequently, there has been vacillation in policy and confusion over such matters as when the question of recognition arises, under what conditions (if any) it should be granted, and what it means once granted. The confusion is reflected in policy statements issued by foreign ministries and the State Department, in press accounts, and in the reaction of the man on the street. Often the question whether to recognize a new government creates strong emotion among average citizens, as it did in the case of the Maoist government in the People's Republic of China.

Practice over two centuries has not established whether recognition of a foreign government constitutes approval of that government. Because the United States utilized recognition as a policy tool on many occasions and granted quick recognition to regimes it favored, the impression was created that recognition connoted approval of the new government, its policies, and perhaps the manner in which it came to power. This approbatory connotation was reinforced by instances where the United States withheld recognition because it disapproved of a new government or the manner in which it gained power, such as the refusal to recognize the Soviet Union for some sixteen years after the Russian Revolution. The U.S. Department of State and most academic texts take the position that recognition does not constitute approval of a new regime, but as late as 1969 the U.S. Senate felt it necessary to pass a resolution to that effect in order to dispel popular confusion.[1]

Similarly, there is dispute over whether a state must accord recognition to a new government once it is in effective control; and if not, what limits exist on the conditions an outside state may set in return for recognition.[2] For example, may a state condition recognition on a return to constitutional government, on agreement to honor international obligations, or in return for economic concessions?

Opinions differ sharply on the scope of one nation's interest in a change of government in another. Most third world nations contend that anything more than a *pro forma* inquiry into a change of government constitutes intervention in that state's domestic affairs. They have charged that developed states have used recognition to extract unfair economic advantages and to interfere in their domestic political processes by passing on the acceptability of leaders, setting election timetables, and so on. In their efforts to halt such practices, the developing nations have introduced a new approach, the Estrada Doctrine, that eliminates the recognition of foreign governments from diplomatic practice.[3] Developed states, on the other hand, have often argued that recognition of a new government is a matter within the discretion of the recognizing state, which, therefore, may set

---

[1] U.S. Congress, Senate, Committee on Foreign Relations, *Hearings on Senate Resolution 205*, 91st Congress, 1st session, June 17, 1969, p. 8.

[2] See, for example, Hersh Lauterpacht, *Recognition in International Law* (Cambridge, England: Cambridge University Press, 1947), pp. 87–97, for the proposition that states have a legal obligation to recognize new governments. See John Foster Dulles, "Our Politics toward Communism in China," in U.S. Department of State, *Bulletin*, vol. 37 (July 1957), pp. 91, 93–94, for the proposition that the decision to recognize a new government is basically a political decision.

[3] Marjorie M. Whiteman, *Digest of International Law*, vol. 2 (Washington, D.C.: Department of State, 1963), pp. 84–85.

whatever conditions it wishes in return for recognition.[4] These two perspectives on the recognition of governments that come to power through extraconstitutional means reflect not only significant differences on the role of recognition in international affairs, but also profound differences in attitude toward the relationship of sovereign nations.

When it appears that a change of government has occurred in a foreign state, outside states are faced with several major questions:

(1) Does a question of recognition of the new government arise?
(2) If so, what criteria should be used to determine whether to grant recognition to the new government?
(3) What effect would recognizing the new government have?

What Raises the Question of Recognition?

Normally a state does not concern itself legally with a change of government in another state. When a change of government occurs in a foreign state that is in accord with the domestic law of that state, the legal relationship between the two governments remains unaffected. For example, Great Britain does not recognize a new government in the United States whenever a new President is elected.

However, under established principles of international law, the legal relationship between two states is affected if a government assumes power in a manner that violates domestic law. When such a change of government occurs, the question of recognition of the new government is said to arise.[5]

The line between a lawful and an unlawful change of govern-

---

[4] U.S. Department of State, Memorandum from Green H. Hackworth, legal adviser, Department of State, to Secretary of State Cordell Hull, "Russia vs. Poland," January 29, 1944, cited in Whiteman, *Digest of International Law*, vol. 2, pp. 5–6.

[5] Though the two are sometimes confused, recognition of a foreign government that comes to power through extraconstitutional means differs from the recognition of a new state. Recognition as a state is accorded to an entity having a defined area and population under the control of a government that has the capacity to engage in foreign relations. Once a state is accorded recognition, it retains its identity in spite of any change that may take place in its internal organization and government, however radical.

Another source of confusion, especially in recent years, has been the relationship between recognition and diplomatic relations. Recognition does not necessarily mean that diplomatic relations will be established or reestablished with the foreign state, although such is normally the case. In recent years, the United States has to some degree merged the two concepts in practice in its attempt to deemphasize recognition. Whiteman, *Digest of International Law*, vol. 2, p. 3.

ment is not always clear, and problems may arise in determining whether a particular change of government raises the question of recognition.

Unlawful changes of government occur in a variety of ways. In perhaps the most extreme case, a revolution may occur in which the social, economic, and political institutions of a state are radically altered. In such a case, there can be no doubt that the change violates the existing domestic law of the state.

Far more common is the military coup d'etat. In the classic case, the military, dissatisfied for one reason or another with the existing government, may take power, killing, imprisoning, or exiling the head of government and members of the cabinet or ruling body. The overt seizure of power is often followed by the formation of a military junta to rule the country until elections are held, or for an indefinite period. As with the case of revolution, when the military seizes power overtly by taking to the streets, there can be little question but that the change of government violates the domestic law of the state, and therefore raises a question of recognition of the new government.

In other cases, it may not be so clear that a change of government is extraconstitutional. For example, the military may bring pressure and cause the resignation of the existing government without an overt show of force. The military may then assume power, commonly with the legislature's approval, which the legislature may or may not have the constitutional authority to bestow.

A similarly questionable change of government occurs when the president is replaced by the vice-president instead of a military junta, but the change is brought about by duress. Here the form of domestic law may be preserved but not the substance. The vice-president who assumes power may be merely a figurehead. In such situations the problems for an outside state in determining whether the question of recognition is raised are patent.

In other cases, it may not even be clear that a change of government has occurred, at least in a formal sense. For example, the military may in fact assume power but leave the head of state and perhaps the head of government in office as figureheads. In such cases outside states are confronted with a difficult choice—whether to accept the action at face value and conclude that no question of recognition arises because no formal change of government has occurred, or to look behind the form and run the risk that their judgments will be attacked as intervention in the domestic affairs of a sovereign state.

Political forces govern the practice of most states when confronted with such situations. For example, in responding to military coups in Latin America in recent years, the United States fairly consistently has refused to make a close inquiry into changes of government, fearing charges of intervention and wishing to maintain relations with as little disturbance as possible.

Neither the United States nor other states has developed guidelines to determine just when the question of recognition is raised. Indeed, this is probably impossible given the differences in the domestic laws of the various states and the great variance in factual circumstances. The decision, therefore, is basically ad hoc with the political interests of the recognizing state outweighing the technical violation of the other state's domestic law.

States may avoid the recognition question entirely simply by deciding that a change has been in accordance with domestic law. This normally occurs when an outside state wishes merely to continue relations with the new government or to maintain a low profile for political reasons.

Criteria for the Grant of Recognition

The decision to recognize a foreign government that comes to power through extraconstitutional means usually involves an interesting and often subtle interplay between the principles of international law and international politics. The interplay is no less interesting merely because political forces often overshadow legal principles.

Some scholars have argued that the decision to recognize a new government is a wholly legal decision.[6] Most policy makers have taken the opposite view, contending that the decision to recognize is political and within the discretion of the recognizing state.[7] In practice, the majority of states blend both law and politics into their decision.

The three major approaches to recognition that have developed in the past two centuries reflect this interplay, and each has its own set of criteria for determining whether to grant recognition. The three are: (1) the traditional approach, (2) the Estrada Doctrine, and (3) the Tobar or Betancourt Doctrine.

Traditional Approach. Under the traditional approach, a state considering recognition first seeks to determine:

(1) whether the government is in de facto control of the territory and in possession of the machinery of the state;

---

[6] Lauterpacht, *Recognition in International Law*, pp. 87–97.

[7] Senate, Committee on Foreign Relations, *Hearings on S. Res. 205*, pp. 8–17.

(2) whether the government has the consent of the people, without substantial resistance to its administration, that is, whether there is public acquiescence in the authority of the government; and

(3) whether the new government has indicated its willingness to comply with its obligations under treaties and international law.[8]

The first criterion is fundamental and by no means limited to the traditional approach. States seldom recognize a new government, at least openly, that is not in effective control of the territory and the machinery of the state.[9] Such action would constitute "premature recognition" and would be considered intervention in the domestic affairs of the state.[10] While the principle is uncontroverted, in practice, when the political interests of the recognizing state favor the new government, the question of effective control may be finessed. The recognition of the Yemen government by the United States in 1962, and the grant of recognition by Hitler and Mussolini to the Franco regime in Spain before Franco had gained control, are examples of such premature recognition.

The second criterion—the consent of the people—is more controversial. In most instances such consent is assumed from popular acquiescence in the assumption of power by the new government. A State Department official, testifying before the Senate Foreign Relations Committee in 1969, explained the United States practice this way:

> CHAIRMAN. With the consent or the acquiescence, which do you mean, or do you mean both?
>
> MR. ALDRICH. Well, I think this is something that can mean different things to different people. We have had this ambiguity since Jefferson referred to "the will of the nation substantially declared."
>
> CHAIRMAN. If it is so ambiguous and difficult, is it really a significant consideration then?
>
> MR. ALDRICH. I think it has been in some cases.
>
> CHAIRMAN. But is it under your present policy?
>
> MR. ALDRICH. I think our present policy is more concerned with the acquiescence rather than the declaration of the will of the people. I think that what we have done in recent years

---

[8] Whiteman, *Digest of International Law*, vol. 2, pp. 72–73.

[9] Green Hackworth, *Digest of International Law*, vol. 1 (Washington, D.C.: Department of State, 1962), pp. 174–192.

[10] Lauterpacht, *Recognition in International Law*, p. 94.

shows a far greater concern with deciding whether the particular government involved has effective control and is not sitting on top of an imminent revolution, but does in fact govern with the acquiescence of the people. We have not generally concerned ourselves with asking, would the people, if given a free plebiscite, endorse that change of government.

CHAIRMAN. In other words, the present policy which, as you say, is established policy, does not require that they be a fully developed democracy in which the people have elected their government?

MR. ALDRICH. I would say that the present policy would like to see that happen but that there are a number of cases in recent years in which we have not insisted on that before recognizing a new government or engaging in diplomatic relations.[11]

The present approach of most states is to interpret the criterion "consent of the people" to mean acquiescence of the people to the new government.

Policy makers have found that in many coups d'etat the concept of actual consent is meaningless. As one State Department official stated:

> Most coups occur in less developed countries which have predominantly illiterate and politically dormant populations. The coup is usually quick, bloodless, and effective. Moreover, such changes in government usually occur in one-party states, and take the form of one elite replacing another elite, political or military. In such circumstances the popular will remains largely irrelevant. In the absence of a popular revolution or a clear division of allegiance within the country, the consent or acquiescence of the population must as a practical matter be taken for granted.[12]

The third criterion under the traditional approach, the willingness to fulfill international obligations, finds its origins in United States practice in the last half of the nineteenth century when the Department of State used the standard to extract guarantees for U.S. investments in unstable Caribbean and Latin American states.[13] Today it is largely a *pro forma* requirement; new regimes that seize power usually announce as a matter of course that they will honor all international obligations.

---

[11] Senate, Committee on Foreign Relations, *Hearings on S. Res. 205*, p. 10.

[12] U.S. Department of State, Office of the Legal Adviser, Memorandum, June 1, 1971.

[13] Lauterpacht, *Recognition in International Law*, pp. 109–114.

Once the three basic criteria under the traditional approach are met, the outside state normally must make a political judgment whether recognition would be in its best interest. In making this political decision, it usually will consider

> the existence or non-existence of evidence of foreign intervention in the establishment of the new regime; the political orientation of the government and its leaders; evidence of intention to observe democratic principles, particularly the holding of elections; the attitude of the new government toward private investment and economic improvement. Importantly, also, the interest of peoples, as distinguished from governments, is of concern. These, and other criteria, depending upon the international situation at the time, have been considered, with varying weight.[14]

One might fairly characterize the traditional approach to recognition as flexible and pragmatic. Each decision to recognize is somewhat ad hoc, with the political interests of the recognizing state the major consideration. In many cases the recognizing state may perceive little national interest in a particular change of government, hence downplaying recognition and resuming relations with as little disturbance as possible. However, if the recognizing state perceives that a significant national interest is involved, under the traditional approach it may bargain with the new regime for free elections, a realization of individual freedoms, economic guarantees, and so forth. In the rare case, a state may withhold recognition for a substantial period of time because the new government refuses to comply with such conditions. For example, the U.S. refusal to recognize the government of Albania after World War II continues to the present.

The Estrada Doctrine. Under the Estrada Doctrine, the recognition of governments that come to power through extraconstitutional means is for all practical purposes eliminated from diplomatic practice. Only new *states* are recognized; when a new *government* comes to power either through constitutional means or otherwise, its relations with outside states remain unchanged.

The doctrine of recognizing only states, and not governments, was first articulated by the Mexican Foreign Minister Don Genaro Estrada in 1930:

> It is a well-known fact that some years ago Mexico suffered, as few nations have, from the consequences of that doctrine, which allows foreign governments to pass upon the

---

[14] Whiteman, *Digest of International Law*, vol. 2, p. 73.

legitimacy or illegitimacy of the regime existing in another country, with the result that situations arise in which the legal qualifications or national status of governments or authorities are apparently made subject to the opinion of foreigners.

Ever since the Great War, the doctrine of so-called recognition has been applied in particular to the nations of this continent, although in well-known cases of change of regime occurring in European countries the governments of the nations have not made express declarations of recognition; consequently, the system has been changing into a special practice applicable to the Latin American Republics.

After a very careful study of the subject, the Government of Mexico has transmitted instructions to its ministers or Chargés d'Affaires in the countries affected by the recent political crises, informing them that the Mexican government is issuing no declarations in the sense of grants of recognition, since that nation considers that such a course is an insulting practice and one which, in addition to the fact that it offends the sovereignty of other nations, implies that judgment of some sort may be passed upon the internal affairs of those nations by other governments, inasmuch as the latter assume, in effect, an attitude of criticism, when they decide, favorably or unfavorably, as to the legal qualifications of foreign regimes.[15]

The Estrada Doctrine embraces the principle of unfettered national sovereignty and rejects interference with the domestic affairs of one state by another through the granting or withholding of recognition. States that have adopted the Estrada Doctrine often say they recognize states, not governments; however, as a practical matter, many states depart from the doctrine whenever they perceive a major political advantage in using the recognition instrument.

A substantial number of states have adopted the Estrada Doctrine, either officially or in practice. In response to the Department of

---

[15] The statement continues: "Therefore, the Government of Mexico confines itself to the maintenance or withdrawal, as it may deem advisable, of its diplomatic agents, and to the continued acceptance, also when it may deem advisable, of such similar accredited diplomatic agents as the respective nations may have in Mexico; and in so doing, it does not pronounce judgment, either precipitately or *a posteriori* regarding the right of foreign nations to accept, maintain or replace their governments or authorities. Naturally, in so far as concerns the usual formulas for accrediting and receiving agents and for the exchange of signed letters of Heads of Government and Chancellors, the Mexican Government will continue to use the same formulas accepted up to the present time by international law and diplomatic law" (Whiteman, *Digest of International Law*, vol. 2, pp. 85–86).

State's 1969 survey, thirty-one states indicated that they had abandoned traditional recognition policies and substituted the Estrada
Doctrine or some equivalent by which they accepted whatever government was in effective control without raising the issue of recognition. Among the states accepting the Estrada Doctrine were Mexico,
France, Finland, Turkey, Germany, Indonesia, and Peru.[16]

The Tobar Doctrine. The Tobar or Betancourt Doctrine stands in direct contrast to the Estrada Doctrine. It attempts to encourage democratic and constitutional government by refusing to recognize any
government that comes to power through extraconstitutional means
until a free election is held and new leaders elected. One writer has
noted: "If the Estrada Doctrine mode of approach assumed automatic
recognition of new governments, then it might be said that, for practical purposes, the Tobar Doctrine implied automatic nonrecognition."[17] This doctrine is often criticized for its substantial interference
with the domestic political processes of sovereign states, and because
it bars revolutionary change as a method to overthrow even corrupt
and despotic governments.

The Tobar Doctrine was first developed by a foreign minister
of Ecuador, and was embodied in a treaty signed in 1907 by five
Central American republics. A 1923 treaty went further and barred
recognition—even if the people constitutionally approved the change
—if the choice of headship or vice-headship fell upon a person con-
nected with the coup d'etat or revolution.

The Tobar Doctrine never has enjoyed widespread acceptance;
however, it did not vanish following the termination of the 1923
treaty. In 1963, the governments of Venezuela and Costa Rica attempted to persuade the governments of the Americas to adopt the
Tobar Doctrine through a resolution submitted to a meeting of foreign
ministers.[18] Although the attempt failed, some states adopted the
doctrine unilaterally, including Venezuela and Costa Rica, which applied the doctrine for several years.

Effect of Recognition. Just as there has been no agreement on the
proper approach to recognition, there is uncertainty and disagreement
over the effect of recognition once granted. In short, what does it
mean to "recognize" a new government?

---

[16] See Appendix A.

[17] Martin Needler, "United States Recognition Policy and the Peruvian Case,"
Inter-American Economic Affairs, vol. 16 (Spring 1963), pp. 61, 67.

[18] Whiteman, *Digest of International Law*, vol. 2, pp. 85–86. Guatemala introduced a similar resolution in 1945 that also failed (p. 84).

As Professor Stephen Schwebel has written, the simple answer is that recognition of foreign governments, for all its long history and frequent use, has little substantive content. Governments deal with each other, sometimes extensively, without recognizing one another. They may negotiate and conclude treaties with governments they do not recognize. They may sit in international or regional organizations with other governments they do not recognize. In fact, they may trade with governments they do not recognize.[19] On the other hand, one state may recognize the government of another and yet have no diplomatic relations with that state, even interdicting trade, limiting travel, and maintaining all intercourse with that state through a third party.[20]

The current relations between the United States and the People's Republic of China on the one hand, and until recently Cuba on the other, illustrate the lack of substantive content in the recognition of foreign governments. The United States recognizes the government of Fidel Castro, but until recently it interdicted trade and limited travel, maintaining no diplomatic ties with Cuba. In contrast, although the United States does not recognize the government of the People's Republic of China, a considerable relationship has developed between the two states. Ambassadors have been exchanged and "liaison offices" established in each state. The President of the United States was received as a head of state by the Chinese government. Cultural exchanges have occurred and trade is now lawful between the two states. Both sit on the Security Council of the United Nations. This relationship was established not only while the United States did not recognize the Maoist government but while it recognized another, that of Chiang Kai-chek, as the government of China.[21]

One might logically inquire why states attach importance to a concept that has so little substantive content. The answer appears to be that the importance attached to recognition derives in part from the weight of tradition and in part from the sense of legitimacy recognition confers. And because states granting or receiving recognition perceive the act as important, they have made it a precondition for other actions that do have inherent significance, such as the continuance of aid or the resumption of diplomatic relations.

The main importance of recognition over the years has been political. Recognition has served as a rough initial indicator of a state's

---

[19] Stephen M. Schwebel, "Is the 'Recognition' of Governments Obsolete?" *Washington Post*, February 23, 1972, p. A15.
[20] Ibid.
[21] Ibid.

attitude toward a new actor on the international political scene and of the recognizing state's values and priorities in international affairs.

If a state feels strongly about constitutional government and democratic rule it may refuse recognition until a new government promises to hold elections. If a state wishes to contest vigorously the spread of an ideology it may refuse to recognize governments of that persuasion that come to power. Or if a state wishes to protect the economic interests of its citizens in the foreign state it may condition recognition on economic or investment guarantees from the new government.

On the other hand, if a state desires to protect national sovereignty, or combat intervention in its internal affairs, it may adopt the Estrada Doctrine and reject the political use of recognition entirely.

No one disputes that states repeatedly have used recognition to advance their political interests in the course of the past two centuries. The controversy concerns whether recognition has been effective in advancing the interests of the recognizing state, and if so, whether it is a legitimate political instrument.

1
HISTORICAL BACKGROUND, 1780-1960

Obscurity shrouds the precise origins of the concept of recognition of foreign governments. However, recognition finds its general beginnings in the political doctrines of the European monarchies and the rise of the modern nation-state.

The doctrine of the divine right of kings was paramount in the late Middle Ages in Europe and the sovereignty of the king was identified with the sovereignty of the state. The king was the "chosen of God" and thus the only legitimate ruler. From this basic premise sprang the concept of legitimacy which provided that any government that came to power in a state depended for its legality not upon de facto control, but upon compliance with the established legal order of the state.[1]

Legitimacy was first invoked on behalf of monarchical governments and reached its zenith in the period following the French Revolution when the European monarchies banded together and determined not to recognize a government created in open revolt. Diplomats at the Congress of Vienna in 1814–1815 invoked the doctrine in their attempts to restore monarchical regimes to power. The Quadruple Alliance formed during the Congress of Vienna likewise provided that sovereignty could not be acquired by an act of conquest. Thus, the great powers hoped to defeat any revolutionary attempts to upset the status quo.

It was within this conservative historical context that the American Revolution occurred. Quite clearly, the United States, born of revolution, could not invoke legitimacy to prevent popular changes of

---

[1] U.S. Department of State, *The Problem of Recognition in American Foreign Policy*, Research Project 174, Division of Historical Policy Research, August 1950, p. 8.

government in foreign states. In fact, the Declaration of Independence had as one of its primal features the right of the people to overthrow an unjust government.

Therefore, it came to the first secretary of state, Thomas Jefferson, to develop and put into practice a revolutionary new theory of recognition to counter the theory of legitimacy, one that gave effect to the consent of the governed.[2] Jefferson developed what came to be known as the de facto theory of recognition, which holds that any government in effective control of a state and representing the will of the people should be accorded recognition. The European monarchies regarded Jefferson's idea as an open encouragement to revolution.

The de facto theory flowed inexorably from Jefferson's general political philosophy, the cornerstones of which were popular sovereignty and the right to revolution. Jefferson, a follower of the social contract theory espoused by John Locke, believed that government was based on the consent of the people and that the people retained a right to abolish any unjust or unrepresentative government and establish one that would represent their will. The step from this belief to the de facto theory of recognition is a short one. One historian has commented:

> Thomas Jefferson is rightly considered the author of many of the cardinal principles of United States foreign policy. No doctrine, however, bears more deeply the imprint of his political thinking than does our recognition policy. Indeed, so far removed were his doctrines from the accepted canons of international law, and even from the recent example of the recognition of the colonies by the French government, that it is impossible to trace any relationship between the two. We are obliged to conclude, therefore, that the ideas developed by Jefferson relative to the de facto principle of recognition were of his own invention and in no way connected with previous international precedents.[3]

Jefferson first applied the principle in 1792, upon the fall of the French monarchy, when he instructed the American ambassador in France:

> It accords with our principles to acknowledge any Government to be rightful which is formed by the will of the

---

[2] Julius Goebel, Jr., *The Recognition Policy of the United States* (New York: Columbia University, 1915).

[3] Ibid., pp. 98–99.

nation, substantially declared. The late government [set up in France by the Revolution of 1789] was of this kind, and was accordingly acknowledged by all the branches of ours; so any alteration of it which shall be made by the will of the nation, substantially declared, will doubtless be acknowledged in like manner.[4]

In later instructions to the ambassador, Jefferson elaborated on the theme:

> . . . We surely can not deny to any nation that right whereon our own Government is founded—that every one may govern itself according to whatever form it pleases, and change these forms at its own will; and that it may transact its business with foreign nations through whatever organ it thinks proper, whether King, convention, assembly, committee, President, or anything else that it may choose. The will of the nation is the only thing essential to be regarded.[5]

Jefferson's ideas on recognition, enunciated in the above instructions, became the foundation of American recognition policy. Under Jefferson's test, recognition was granted to a new government, whatever the origin of the government, on the basis of two criteria:

(1) The government to be recognized should be in actual control of the entire governmental authority.

(2) The government to be recognized should represent the will of the nation, substantially declared.[6]

During the early nineteenth century the United States became the foremost champion of the de facto theory of recognition. In developing recognition policy in this period the foreign policy decision makers stressed the acceptance of the government de facto and assumed that the acquiescence of the people signified the will of the people.[7] Thus, for practical purposes, U.S. recognition policy was virtually automatic, turning solely on a question of fact—did the new government have effective control?[8] If it did, recognition was granted.[9]

---

[4] Ibid., quoting Jefferson, *Works* (Washington edition) vol. 3, p. 500.

[5] Department of State, *Problem of Recognition in American Foreign Policy*, p. 7.

[6] Ibid.

[7] Ibid., p. 9.

[8] Scholars have argued that the doctrine of nonintervention was a historical development that subsequently justified the de facto theory of recognition but was not, as some have said, the basis for the development of the de facto theory itself. Goebel, *Recognition Policy of the United States*, p. 113.

[9] Department of State, *Problem of Recognition in American Foreign Policy*, p. 15.

Whatever its democratic sympathies, the United States normally followed the simple formula that the government de facto was equally de jure.[10]

Role of Congress

Jefferson envisioned recognition as a function of the executive branch of government, and this is largely how the practice of granting recognition to new governments developed. Congress did however play a limited role in recognition in the early nineteenth century.

In 1811, the House of Representatives passed a resolution claiming the prerogative of empowering the President to accord recognition by appropriating money to pay diplomatic agents to be assigned to the new powers. Similarly, Henry Clay argued for the proposition that Congress could grant recognition to new states or governments, reasoning that by passing a statute regulating universal intercourse, recognition would be automatically conferred:

> This House unquestionably has a right to recognize in the exercise of the Constitutional power of Congress to regulate foreign commerce. . . . Suppose for example we passed an act to regulate trade between the United States and Buenos Aires [sic]; the existence of the nation would therefore be recognized as we could not regulate trade with a nation which does not exist.[11]

Clay made further attempts in 1818 and 1836 to gain at least concurrent control for Congress of the power to recognize states and governments. The first attempt was through an amendment to an appropriation bill to include the sum of $18,000 for one year's salary of a minister to the United Provinces of Rio de la Plata and to pay the cost of maintaining an embassy. Clay felt that passage of the amendment would constitute recognition of the new state.

In 1836 Clay introduced a resolution stating that the inde-

---

[10] Ibid. A report in 1836 by Senator Henry Clay of the Foreign Relations Committee reflects this noninterventionist philosophy: "The policy which has hitherto guided the Government of the United States in respect to new powers has been to act on the fact of their existence, without regard to their origin, whether that has been by the subversion of pre-existing Government or by the violent or voluntary separation of one from another part of a common nation" (ibid., p. 16).

[11] *Annals of Congress*, 15th Congress, 1st sess., vol. 2, p. 1499, quoted in Charles L. Cochran, "The Recognition of States and Governments by President John F. Kennedy: An Analysis" (Ph.D. diss., Tufts University, 1969), pp. 33–34. Clay here was concerned with the recognition of new states, not with the recognition of a government within a state. However, the legal rationale would seem to apply to recognition of new governments.

pendence of Texas should be acknowledged by the United States whenever satisfactory information was received that it had a government capable of performing the duties and fulfilling the obligations of an independent nation. This resolution passed the Senate and was endorsed by President Jackson:

> It will always be considered consistent with the spirit of the Constitution, and most safe, that it, the spirit of recognition, should be exercised, when probably leading to war, with a previous understanding with that body by whom war can alone be declared, and by whom all the provisions for sustaining its perils must be furnished.[12]

Modification of De Facto Principle

There was some modification of the de facto principle before the Civil War. In 1848, a number of revolutions occurred in Europe that evoked great sympathy in the United States and altered recognition policy by placing an emphasis on Jefferson's second criterion, the will of the nation, at the expense of the criterion of effective control.

In February 1848, Secretary of State James Buchanan sent an instruction to the U.S. minister in Paris that went beyond the de facto principle and indicated that recognition policy be applied to favor democratic government.[13] The first part of the instruction to the minister paralleled the usual doctrine.

---

[12] John Bassett Moore, *A Digest of International Law*, vol. 1 (Washington, D.C.: Government Printing Office, 1906), p. 99. Congress has on various other occasions commented on its role in the recognition of particular governments or states. In 1864 the Committee on Foreign Affairs in the House of Representatives advanced a resolution that stated: "Congress has a constitutional right to an authoritative voice in declaring and prescribing the foreign policy of the United States as well in the recognition of new Powers as in other matters." (*H. Rep. 129*, 38th Congress, 1st session, p. 156.) In 1897 the Senate Foreign Relations Committee recommended adoption by the Senate of a resolution which stated "that the independence of Cuba be, and the same is hereby, acknowledged by the United States of America." (*Sen. Doc. 231*, 56th Congress, 2nd session, p. 64.) These congressional actions concerned the recognition of a new state. However, Congress also took action on the issue of recognition of governments. In 1919 Senator Fall introduced a resolution that sought the removal of recognition from the Carranza regime in Mexico; in 1922 a resolution was introduced to the effect that "the Senate of the United States favors the recognition of the present Soviet Government in Russia." (*Ibid.*, 67th Congress, 2nd session, p. 6945.) Also with regard to the Soviet government, a resolution was introduced in the House "*directing* the President of the United States to recognize the present government of Russia." (*Ibid.*, 69th Congress, 1st session, p. 8872.) This material was first collected in T. Cole, *The Recognition Policy of the United States since 1901* (Baton Rouge: Louisiana State University, 1928), pp. 12–13.

[13] Department of State, *Problem of Recognition in American Foreign Policy*, pp. 18–19.

In its intercourse with foreign nations the Government of the United States has, from its origin, always recognized *de facto* governments. We recognize the right of all nations to create and reform their political institutions according to their own will and pleasure. We do not go behind the existing Government to involve ourselves in the question of legitimacy. It is sufficient for us to know that a government exists capable of maintaining itself, and then its recognition on our part inevitably follows.

However, Secretary Buchanan then introduced a new factor: "Whilst this is our own settled policy, it does not follow that we can ever be indifferent spectators to the progress of liberty throughout the world, and especially in France."[14] Secretary Buchanan believed that the United States should be the first to recognize the provisional government because of the democratic nature of the new regime. President Polk supported this idea in his message to Congress in 1848. He stated that while the policy of the United States has "ever been that of nonintervention in the domestic affairs of other countries, leaving to each to establish the form of government of its own choice, all U.S. sympathies were on the side of democracy and the new regime."[15]

However if a return to democratic government was not involved, the normal procedure of recognizing any government in control of a state was followed. For example, the traditional policy of recognizing de facto governments was applied with vigor in 1856–1857 in the successive coups in Mexico.[16] During these years there were a number of governmental changes in Mexico. Despite the rapidity of developments the United States recognized each, not concerning itself with the stability of the governments it recognized, much less with a commitment to constitutional government. In May 1856, President Franklin Pierce informed Congress that five successive governments had assumed authority in Mexico in the course of a few months and had been recognized successively by the United States.[17]

---

[14] Ibid., p. 19.

[15] Ibid., pp. 19–22. This principle was followed by President Taylor in recognizing the new regime that resulted from the Hungarian revolution. The same response was used in the revolution of 1848–1849 in Germany, where the Buchanan corollary was used to justify recognizing a de facto government more promptly and enthusiastically than was usual.

[16] Ibid., p. 23.

[17] Ibid. In 1856, in perhaps the most sweeping statement ever made by a U.S. President on adherence to a pure de facto recognition policy, Franklin Pierce said: "It is the established policy of the United States to recognize all governments without question of their source, or organization, or of the means by which the governing persons attain their power. To us it is indifferent whether a successful revolution has been aided by foreign intervention or not; whether insurrection

The Recognition Practice from 1860 to 1913

With the outbreak of the Civil War, American recognition policy became more complex as the United States began increasingly to look to other considerations besides the factual existence of a new government. Factors such as the extent to which the new government represented the will of the nation, the degree of stability which the government possessed, and its willingness to fulfill international obligations, began to play roles in the decision to recognize.[18]

The first signs of a departure from the de facto policy came before the Civil War in the policy of Secretary of State Webster. When Louis Napoleon overthrew the French Republic and became virtual dictator of France in 1851, the United States was faced with a case of de facto control but with a return to conservative, monarchical government. The United States did not extend recognition to the new regime immediately, but waited until a national plebiscite was held. Secretary Webster summarized the U.S. position in a communication to the American diplomatic representative in France:

> Before this reaches you, the election will be over; and if, as is probable, a decided majority of the people should be found to support the President, the course of duty for you will become plain. While we deeply regret the overthrow of popular institutions, yet our ancient ally has still our good wishes for its prosperity and happiness, and we are bound to leave to her the choice of means for the promotion of those ends.[19]

This action by Secretary Webster marked a significant deviation from past recognition practices, one that would appear in later policy. Here the United States waited until elections were held before granting recognition, presumably relying on the second criterion of Jefferson's recognition formula—"the will of the people, substantially declared."

The change in policy heralded by Secretary Webster came to fruition during the 1860s, as a result of the efforts of Secretary of State William Seward, who served under President Lincoln. One of

---

has overthrown existing government and another has been established in its place, according to pre-existing forms, or in a manner adopted for the occasion by those whom we may find in the actual possession of power. It is the more imperatively necessary to apply this rule to the Spanish-American republics, in consideration of the frequent and not seldom anomalous change or organization or administration which they undergo, and the revolutionary nature of most of the changes." Moore, *Digest of International Law*, vol. 1, p. 142.

[18] Department of State, *Problem of Recognition in American Foreign Policy*, p. 24.

[19] Ibid., p. 22.

Seward's tasks was to prevent the recognition of the Confederacy by the great powers of Europe, a task that had an impact on Seward's views on general recognition policy. It was difficult for Seward to follow an automatic, factual policy of recognition while at the same time opposing the right of other nations to recognize the Confederate government.[20]

According to some historians, the principle that Seward developed was based on the fortuitous fact that the Confederate States of America, because of wartime conditions, never convened a popularly chosen Constituent Assembly nor held elections for a legislative body. Seward seized on this historical accident, so it is argued, to develop the principle that only a regularly organized state formally accepted by the people under its jurisdiction merited recognition. In this inauspicious situation some find "the origin of the doctrine that 'free elections' are requisite to a government's recognition by the United States."[21]

A British jurist, Hersh Lauterpacht, more accurately pointed to the real origin of this principle. While Seward did seize upon the anomaly to justify nonrecognition of the Confederacy, statements by Seward, and before him Secretary Webster, reflect a deep concern for the instability pervading Latin America and a growing dissatisfaction with the never-ending line of military dictatorships. The de facto principle advanced by Jefferson was aimed at elevating the will of the people against the encroachments of monarchical legitimism. As Lauterpacht notes, however, when it became apparent that adherence to de facto recognition resulted in substituting the tyranny of ruthless and adventurous dictatorships for that of monarchies, the United States adopted the principle of subsequent legitimation by the people.[22]

In 1862 Seward refused to recognize a new government in Venezuela despite its de facto establishment. Seward indicated there was

> a Revolutionary spirit pervading the republican states on this continent, and that the United States therefore deemed it a duty to discourage that spirit so far as it can be done by standing entirely aloof from all such domestic controversies until, in each case, the state immediately concerned shall

---

[20] Ibid., p. 24. Technically, the recognition of the Confederacy would have been recognition of a new state, not recognition of a new government of an already existing state.

[21] Needler, "United States Recognition Policy and the Peruvian Case," p. 63.

[22] Hersh Lauterpacht, *Recognition in International Law* (Cambridge, England: University Press, 1947), pp. 115–16.

unmistakably prove that the government which claims to represent it is fully accepted and peacefully maintained by the people thereof.[23]

Seward went further in modifying the traditional de facto policy in 1866 by instructing the American minister to Peru not to recognize a revolutionary regime that had seized power: "Revolutions in republican states ought not to be accepted until the people have adopted them by organic law with the solemnities which would seem sufficient to guarantee their stability and permanency."[24] Seward felt that the de facto recognition policy stimulated unrest by making it too easy for a self-seeking group of revolutionaries to obtain governmental status.[25] Therefore in such situations recognition should be withheld until there was evidence of a "formal acquiescence and acceptance of the new regime by the people."[26] The Seward argument bears a marked similarity to that advanced by the monarchies of Jefferson's time.

Later administrations did not adopt the Seward view wholeheartedly. Nonetheless, the United States did apply Seward's criteria to various coups in Latin America in the latter half of the nineteenth century. In 1880, the Department of State instructed the American minister to Peru to recognize a new regime in Peru if it was "supported by the character and intelligence of Peru and is really endeavoring to restore constitutional government." In 1883, the United States recognized a new regime in Peru only after the new president was confirmed in office by a representative assembly. In 1885, after one government had fallen from power, the Department of State announced that the new president would be recognized "when his authority shall have been confirmed by the Peruvian people."[27]

Willingness to Honor International Obligations. Another criterion—the fulfillment of international obligations—began to receive increasing emphasis in American recognition policy following the Civil

---

[23] Department of State, *Problem of Recognition in American Foreign Policy*, p. 25.

[24] Ibid., p. 26.

[25] Ibid., p. 24. Seward followed the same policy in 1868 in the coup d'etat in Peru. Seward explained that the United States did not question the right of any nation to change its constitution, even by force in rare instances, but he did insist that the new government be sanctioned by the formal acquiescence and acceptance of the people. U.S. Department of State, *Diplomatic Correspondence*, vol. 2 (1868), p. 864.

[26] Department of State, *Problem of Recognition in American Foreign Policy*, pp. 27–28.

[27] Ibid.

War.[28] Technically, this was not a new criterion, since the principle was accepted that the obligations of a state are not affected by changes of government.[29] However, in the years after the Civil War, the United States would not assume that any government in actual control would acknowledge or fulfill its international obligations, that is, would honor treaties and agreements entered into by the preceding regime.

The reason for the increased U.S. interest in this factor, and its application to recognition policy, lay in the growing economic interests of the United States in foreign lands. In the second half of the nineteenth century the United States enjoyed a period of sustained economic growth and expansion, and it became a major creditor nation. Recognition policy was altered to serve this new interest.

Many of the states in which Americans invested substantially suffered from chronic political instability and deep-seated poverty. This combination resulted in frequent defaults on government bonds and other instruments, making such investments risky. In an attempt to protect American holdings, the United States relied on recognition as a bargaining weapon and increasingly insisted on evidence that a new government would pay its debts and respect foreign investment.[30] In its zeal to protect legitimate interests, the United States repeatedly overstepped the bounds of legitimate action and actually took direct control of the finances of Haiti and the Dominican Republic in order to ensure the sanctity of American investments. Recognition of new governments was a handmaiden of the overall drive to protect U.S. financial interests.[31]

For example, General Guzman Blanco seized power in Venezuela and was recognized promptly by Brazil, Great Britain, France, Germany, Italy, and Spain. The United States withheld recognition, even though Blanco was in unquestioned control of the country and its governmental machinery. Secretary of State Evarts "thought it best to defer intercourse" until the United States could assure itself that

---

[28] A distinction must be drawn between the ability to honor international obligations and the *willingness* to honor them. While at various times the United States has insisted on both, the major problem arises over emphasis on willingness to honor international obligations. The ability to honor international obligations is merely one aspect of the requirement of effective control of the governmental machinery.

[29] Department of State, *Problem of Recognition in American Foreign Policy*, p. 29.

[30] William Neumann, *Recognition of Governments in the Americas* (Washington, D.C.: Foundation for Foreign Affairs, 1947), p. 7.

[31] President Hayes's annual message to Congress in 1877 is sometimes cited as the first instance of reliance on this criterion in United States recognition policy. However, as early as 1836, Henry Clay had referred to the ability to fulfill international obligations as a criterion for the recognition of a state.

such a step will not only rest on the popular will of Venezuela but will also be beneficial to the relations between the
United States and that country. *Good faith in the observance
of international obligations is the first essential towards the
maintenance of such relations.* At present there is no indication that any change for the better has taken place, either as
regards the payment of the indemnity installments, now for
several months in default, or the security of the rights of
citizens of the United States sojourning in Venezuela.[32]
[Emphasis added.]

Similarly, in 1877, the United States withheld recognition from
a new government in Mexico because of "occurrences on the Rio
Grande border" that raised questions about the willingness of the
new regime to honor its international obligations.[33]

These incidents ultimately subsided and formal recognition was
granted the next year (May 1878).

The emphasis on fulfillment of international obligations grew
more marked at the turn of the century during the presidencies of
Roosevelt and Taft. Roosevelt utilized recognition policy as "a means
of enforcing his demands—a means to see that American interests
were protected and advanced."[34] Taft, if anything, was more aggressive than Roosevelt in protecting American financial interests. As one
historian commented: "If Roosevelt had been painstaking in looking
after the rights of Americans in foreign states and especially in Latin
America, Taft was actually aggressive in attempting to aid American
financiers in those regions."[35]

The emphasis on international obligations was limited almost ex-
clusively to the Latin American area. As one historian commented in
regard to recognition of a new government in Serbia in 1903:

The fact that no special mention was made of international
obligations in the correspondence leading up to the recognition of the government headed by Karageorgevitch does
not signify by any means that this instance furnishes an exception to a rather well established rule. American financiers
had not found in Serbia the rich opportunity for investment
that they had found in Latin America, and American citizens
had not yet begun to travel or reside in this part of the
world in any numbers. *De facto* control only was necessary in

---

[32] Cole, *The Recognition Policy of the United States since 1901*, p. 32, citing;
Moore, *Digest of International Law*, vol. 1 (1906), p. 50.

[33] Department of State, *Problem of Recognition in American Foreign Policy*, p. 30.

[34] Cole, *Recognition Policy of the United States since 1901*, p. 43.

[35] Ibid., pp. 44–45.

Serbia. De facto control and especially the willingness to fulfill their international responsibilities (which were usually specified by reference to American concessions) and claims were both essential in Latin-American states.[36]

Recognition Practice toward Coups d'Etat in Central America. Principles different from those applied to other states governed the grant of recognition to states in Central America in the early part of the twentieth century. The general instability in Latin America was especially pronounced in Central America and there was almost continual warfare in the region in the early twentieth century.[37] President Roosevelt arranged a conference in 1907 to consider the problem, and several conventions were agreed upon, including an annex on recognition policy that was agreed to by Costa Rica, Guatemala, Honduras, Nicaragua, and El Salvador. The annex provided:

> ARTICLE 1. The government of the high contracting parties shall not recognize any other government which may come into power in any of the five Republics as a consequence of coup d'etat, or of a revolution against the recognized government, so long as the freely elected representatives of the people thereof, have not constitutionally reorganized the country.
>
> ARTICLE 2. No government of Central America shall in case of civil war intervene in favor of or against the government of the country where the struggle is taking place.
>
> ARTICLE 3. The Governments of Central America, in the first place, are recommended to endeavor to bring about, by the means at their command, a constitutional reform in the sense of prohibiting the re-election of the President of a republic, where such prohibition does not exist, secondly to adopt all measures necessary to effect a complete guarantee of the principle of alternation in power.[38]

The United States was not a party to the treaty but agreed to follow the policy enunciated in the annex in granting or withholding recognition to new governments in the five states of Central America.[39] Thus the criterion of explicit popular support or subsequent ratification by election which had before been invoked in an ad hoc manner was placed on a formal juridical footing in Central America.

---

[36] Ibid., pp. 83–85.

[37] Raymond Leslie Buell, "The United States and Central American Stability," *Foreign Policy Reports*, vol. 7 (1931), p. 161.

[38] Department of State, *Problem of Recognition in American Foreign Policy*, pp. 28–29.

[39] Ibid., p. 29.

The 1907 treaty was replaced in 1923 by a considerably more drastic version. Under the treaty of 1907 the revolutionary forces could retain power and legalize their position by means of elections. This opportunity was foreclosed by the treaty of 1923 which forbade the leader of the revolutionary forces from assuming control of the government even if he won a free election following the coup and commanded strong popular support.[40]

Both the 1907 and the 1923 treaties had repeated application. Coups occurred in all the Central American countries. Revolutions or coups d'etat occurred in Nicaragua in 1909, 1912, and 1926. Honduras experienced coups in 1911, 1919, 1924, and 1931. General Tinoco assumed power in Costa Rica by extraconstitutional means in 1917. Guatemalan governments were overthrown three times in this period, first in the Cabrera coup in 1920, next in the Herrara coup in 1921, and finally in the Orellano coup in 1930. A coup occurred in El Salvador in 1931.[41]

In each coup, the United States ostensibly followed the treaty in force at that time. However, the actual policy followed by the United States government varied considerably depending on the political forces involved. For example, President Taft and Secretary of State Knox were strongly opposed to President Zelaya of Nicaragua and favored the coup against him in 1909. To aid the anti-Zelaya forces, President Taft refused to allow anyone associated with Zelaya to stand for the presidential election. Similarly, President Wilson was bitterly opposed to General Tinoco, who assumed power in Costa Rica in 1917. Thus, despite the fact that Tinoco met the requirements of the 1907 treaty, President Wilson refused to recognize Tinoco's government.[42]

In Nicaragua, the United States recognized Adolfo Diaz as president even though he was an uncle of one of the leaders of the coup against the existing government, an action in violation of the treaty. The United States repeated the violation in 1926 when it recognized Moncado as president of Nicaragua following the overthrow of Diaz,

---

[40] Secretary of State Stimson outlined United States policy in a statement: " 'It [policy of not recognizing unconstitutional governments] is quite different from the general policy of this country and from the general policy of international law toward the recognition of governments in the world at large.' The reason for adopting a more stringent policy in regard to Central America was that the five governments of that area had agreed to apply the restrictions themselves, 'with the object evidently of discouraging a revolution or coup d'etat within the five Republics.' " Department of State, *Problem of Recognition in American Foreign Policy*, p. 57.

[41] Raymond Leslie Buell, "The United States and Central American Revolutions," *Foreign Policy Reports*, vol. 7 (1931), pp. 187, 201.

[42] Ibid., p. 202.

even though Moncado had led the coup. The failure of the United States to follow either the letter or the spirit of the 1907 and 1923 treaties led to criticism that U.S. policy was not to discourage revolution and coups, the aim of the treaties, but "to maintain in office in Central America presidents answerable to its influence."[43]

The bloodless Tinoco overthrow of the Gonzalez regime in Costa Rica provides a graphic illustration of the deep U.S. involvement in the internal affairs of a Central American country as a result of the 1907 treaty. On January 25, 1917, General Frederico Tinoco overthrew President Alfredo Gonzalez, who claimed that a conflict over an oil concession to American businessmen was the principal cause of the coup. Tinoco nevertheless was initially popular with the people and quickly placed his regime on a constitutional basis. He held elections on April 1, 1917, received an overwhelming majority, and was proclaimed president by the Constitutional Assembly. President Wilson refused to recognize the Tinoco government even though it was eligible under the 1907 treaty. Indeed, the United States hardened its stand and informed Central American governments that recognition of Tinoco would not be "evidence of a friendly feeling toward the United States."[44] Despite this warning, all Central American governments, save Nicaragua, granted recognition as did most South American and European governments.[45] Historians cite two reasons for the U.S. nonrecognition: the doctrine of constitutionalism and Wilson's view that Tinoco had staged the coup at least in part as a result of the actions of American businessmen.

In August 1917 internal problems multiplied, and Tinoco stepped down in favor of Juan Bautista Quiros. The United States refused to recognize Quiros, and he stepped down after twenty days in favor of Francisco Aguilar Barquero, whom the United States said should be the president because he was the third designate elected in 1914 under the 1871 Constitution. This position was outlined by the secretary of state:

> The governmental power should be deposited in the hands of Francisco Aguilar Barquero, successor to the executive power, under the Alfredo Gonzalez regime. Barquero should hold free and open elections for president at earliest possible date. Were this done, it would appear that the necessary legal formalities had been complied with to con-

---

[43] Ibid.

[44] Buell, "The United States and Central American Stability," p. 181.

[45] Ibid., pp. 180–183.

26

stitute a legitimate government worthy of recognition by the Government of the United States.[46]

The U.S. action was bitterly resented in Costa Rica. When Aguilar was elected designate in 1914, his term was only four years; Costa Ricans regarded as ridiculous the argument that he was the "legal" president in 1919.

The Recognition Policy of Woodrow Wilson

President Wilson made significant changes in the traditional recognition doctrine by extending to all Latin America the constitutional criterion that had previously been applied on a formal basis only to the five republics of Central America.

On March 11, 1913, seven days after he assumed office, President Wilson set forth in a public statement the principles for recognition to be followed not only in the case at hand but also in future actions. His statement was a strong endorsement of a policy designed to strengthen constitutional democracy.

> Cooperation is possible only when supported at every turn by the orderly processes of just government based upon law, not upon arbitrary or irregular force. We hold, as I am sure all thoughtful leaders of republican government everywhere hold, that just government rests always upon the consent of the governed, and that there can be no freedom without order based upon law and upon the public conscience and approval. We shall look to make these principles the basis of mutual intercourse, respect, and helpfulness between our sister republics and ourselves. We shall lend our influence of every kind to the realization of these principles in fact and practice, knowing that disorder, personal intrigues, and defiance of constitutional rights weaken and discredit government and injure none so much as the people who are unfortunate enough to have their common life and their common affairs so tainted and disturbed. We can have no sympathy with those who seek to seize the power of government to advance their own personal interests or ambitions.[47]

Wilson's policy was a significant though not total break with past recognition policy. The legitimist criteria of the Central America Treaty of 1907 served as a limited precedent for it as did Secretary

---

[46] Ibid., p. 183.

[47] Hackworth, *Digest of International Law*, vol. 1 (1940), p. 181.

Seward's requirement of explicit popular support. Nonetheless, the Wilson policy marked a strong shift in emphasis.[48]

The Wilson administration utilized recognition as a political sanction to support constitutionalism, particularly in Latin America, and to discourage the overthrow of existing governments. There is an ironic parallel between Wilson's use of recognition to discourage dictators and encourage democracy and the European monarchies' use of recognition to discourage democracy and encourage the monarchical form of government in the eighteenth and nineteenth centuries.[49]

Wilson did not apply this policy often in non-Western Hemisphere changes of government,[50] and even in Latin America he did not invoke it consistently, not applying it to revolutionary governments that seized power in Peru in 1914 and 1919. On the other hand, he did apply it against new regimes in Mexico, the Dominican Republic, Ecuador, Haiti, and Cuba.[51]

Perhaps the primal illustration of the Wilson approach is found in his dealings with General Huerta of Mexico who came to power in 1913. President Wilson stated in August 1913, in instructions to a personal representative who was to negotiate with Mexican authori-

---

[48] Department of State, *Problem of Recognition in American Foreign Policy*, p. 36. One historian commenting on this parallel noted: "Recognition thus came to be used as a means of ensuring democratic regimes, at least in middle America, upon the assumption, presumably, that only such regimes were consonant with the Pan American ideal. The conception of recognition as a moral sanction represented a throwback to the legitimist principle of the eighteenth and early nineteenth centuries. Under that arrangement established governments operated their own club with rules of their own choosing and required applicants for membership to comply with those rules. Those rules were based upon the supposed interests of monarchies and the rights of dynastic succession. That system had been rejected by the young American nations as they took their places in the international community. But in what Baty has called 'this illogical twentieth century' it has been resurrected, not, as formerly, for the purpose of defending monarchy, but rather as a means for promoting democratic or constitutional legitimacy. The actual existence of a regime in power in a state and its continuance in power were not deemed sufficient proof that its power rested upon the consent of the governed." D. Dozier, "Recognition in Contemporary Inter-American Relations," *Journal of Inter-American Studies*, vol. 8 (1966), pp. 322–323.

[49] Ibid., pp. 318, 325.

[50] The most significant issue of recognition to arise in Europe during the Wilson presidency was that occasioned by the overthrow of the provisional government of Russia (under Alexander Kerensky) by the Bolsheviks on November 7, 1917. The provisional government had assumed power upon the abdication of the Tzar of Russia, Nicholas II, on March 7, 1917. It was accorded U.S. recognition on March 20. However, the United States withheld recognition of the new Bolshevik government for sixteen years, until November 16, 1933. The reasons underlying the refusal to recognize are well known, and centered on the Bolshevik unwillingness to honor international obligations and the United States aversion to the revolutionary nature of Communist ideology.

[51] Hackworth, *Digest of International Law*, vol. 1, p. 185.

ties, the conditions he thought necessary for a satisfactory settlement of the recognition question:

(1) An immediate cessation of fighting throughout Mexico, a definite armistice solemnly entered into and scrupulously observed;

(2) Security guaranteed for an early and free election in which all will agree to take part;

(3) The consent of General Huerta to bind himself not to be a candidate for election as President of the Republic at this election; and

(4) The agreement of all parties to abide by the results of the election and cooperate in the most loyal way in organizing and supporting the new administration.[52]

Huerta rejected the conditions. Wilson then maintained his policy of nonrecognition for two-and-one-half years, even after Huerta had been elected by the Mexican people, until Carranza came to power in 1915 and was accorded recognition.[53] Not surprisingly, the Wilsonian recognition policy was criticized, especially by Latin Americans, as placing one state, the United States, in the position of making itself the arbiter over the internal affairs of another, thus violating the principle of nonintervention.

President Wilson generally sought to use recognition as a political weapon to strengthen constitutional government. However, he violated his own ideals on occasion, and attempted to exclude from power certain political leaders the United States did not favor, even after they had been elected. On other occasions he accorded recognition to governments before elections were held if he perceived this to be in the national interest of the United States.

The Recognition Policies of Harding, Coolidge, and Hoover

The decade of the 1920s, and the presidencies of Harding, Coolidge, and Hoover, saw a renewed emphasis on American economic interests. When Harding took office, the question of the recognition of the Obregon regime in Mexico was outstanding. American investors in Mexican oil and mining were concerned with a provision of the Mexi-

---

[52] Department of State, *Problem of Recognition in American Foreign Policy*, p. 38.
[53] The government of Carranza was recognized by the United States when it agreed to honor all contracts and obligations of the government that had been superseded, to protect foreign life and property, to make indemnity for injuries caused by the revolution, to allow religious freedom, and to hold popular elections upon the restoration of peace. Whiteman, *Digest of International Law*, vol. 2, p. 70.

can constitution which separated sub-soil mineral rights from the title to the surface.

Senator Albert Fall, the secretary of the interior under Harding, set out the basic United States position: "So long as I have anything to do with the Mexican question, no government of Mexico will be recognized with my consent, which does not first enter into a written agreement promising to protect American citizens and their property rights in Mexico."[54] Secretary of State Hughes reiterated this position. Nevertheless, President Obregon refused the offer to negotiate, contending that he would accept recognition only on an equal basis with the United States and on terms that did not compromise Mexico's sovereignty. The United States rejected this view and advanced the unique argument that recognition did not fall within the scope of international law but was purely a domestic question. The United States then withheld recognition for two and one-half years, even though all Latin American states had recognized the Obregon government.[55]

The constitutionalist views of President Wilson, while not totally rejected by the Harding and Coolidge administrations, were relegated to a position of less importance in U.S. recognition policy. The administrations of Harding, Coolidge, and Hoover normally accepted the general acquiescence of the people as sufficient and did not require formal evidence of popular support for a government that came to power through extraconstitutional means. The administration of President Hoover in fact explicitly abandoned constitutional legitimism in a statement by Secretary of State Stimson in 1931.[56]

The Recognition Policy of Franklin Roosevelt

Latin America. President Franklin D. Roosevelt indicated from the outset that he favored a return to the "traditional" policy of recognizing new governments primarily on the basis of their de facto

---

[54] Neumann, *Recognition of Governments in the Americas*, pp. 10–11.

[55] Ibid., p. 11. The United States finally extended recognition following a compromise agreement that established a program of indemnification for expropriated land and protected American oil interests in Mexico.

[56] "The present administration has refused to follow the policy of Mr. Wilson and has followed consistently the formal practice of this Government since the days of Jefferson. As soon as it was reported to us, through our diplomatic representatives, that the new governments in Bolivia, Peru, Argentina, Brazil, and Panama were in control of the administrative machinery of the State, with the apparent general acquiescence of their people, and that they are willing and apparently able to discharge their international and conventional obligations, they were recognized by our government." Department of State, *Problem of Recognition in American Foreign Policy*, p. 48.

existence. He retained but deemphasized the requirement that a new government give evidence of its willingness to fulfill international obligations. President Roosevelt and his secretary of state, Cordell Hull, also stressed the need for consultation among American republics before extending recognition to a new government in the Western Hemisphere.[57]

President Roosevelt's Good Neighbor Policy toward Latin America rested on the doctrine of nonintervention. As a corollary, no test of recognition could pass judgment on the constitutionality of the internal processes of foreign governments. In a direct repudiation of the Wilsonian doctrine, President Roosevelt stated in 1933 that he favored a policy of nonintervention and mutual consultation:

> The maintenance of constitutional government in other nations is not a sacred obligation devolving upon the United States alone. The maintenance of law and orderly processes of government in this hemisphere is the concern of each individual nation within its own borders first of all. . . . If and when the failure of orderly processes affects the other nations of the continent it becomes the joint concern of the whole continent in which we are all neighbors.[58]

Despite this general policy, recognition of new regimes in Latin America did not become automatic. Indeed, in the thirteen years of the Roosevelt presidency, recognition of new governments was considered in fifteen instances and significantly delayed or withheld for political purposes on five occasions.[59]

---

[57] Until the 1920s recognition was an unilateral act, completely within the discretion of the recognizing state. The 1920s saw the first halting movement by an international body to consider the issue, and in 1925 there was an attempt by an inter-American judicial body to codify recognition practice. Following this, no further inter-American steps were taken to codify recognition practice or provide for collective recognition action until the 1940s. The recognition issue increasingly became integrated into the general fabric of the developing inter-American system, and acquired procedures not present in recognition policy in other areas of the world. Ibid., p. 66.

[58] Ibid., pp. 67–68.

[59] For example, recognition was withheld for two years in the United States response to the Hernandez Martinez regime in El Salvador which took power in December 1931. When Roosevelt assumed office, the 1923 treaty concerning recognition of new Central American governments was still in effect. Consequently, when General Hernandez Martinez assumed power, the United States took the position that recognition could not be accorded because the assumption of power violated the terms of the 1923 treaty. Martinez had assumed the presidency through military coup d'etat, and the new regime had not been ratified through free elections. Also, Martinez was disqualified from the presidency since he had been minister of war within six months of the coup. In February 1932 the United States rejected a plan to have Martinez deposit the power of the presidency in the first vice-president for six months and reassume the presidency thereafter.

The overall United States attitude toward military coups in Latin America and recognition of the new regimes is perhaps best captured in a telegram from an embassy official concerning the U.S. position on the assumption of power in Ecuador by General Enriquez in 1937:

> A military dictatorship under one guise or another will continue in power in Ecuador for some time to come with possible occasional changes in the supreme chief. The question, therefore, would seem to be the recognition of that form of government which apparently is accepted by the people of Ecuador because (1st) they have no other choice and (2nd) they seem resigned to the fact that constitutional government cannot be had. Accordingly, we shall probably continue to have to deal with this form of government.[60]

Influence of World War II on Recognition Policy. With the outbreak of World War II, the American states established the Inter-American Emergency Advisory Committee for Political Defense for the purpose of studying and coordinating measures for preventing subversive activities that might be harmful to the security of the American republics. The committee in 1943 adopted a Resolution on the Recognition of New Governments Instituted by Force which provided:

> For the duration of the present world conflict they do not proceed to the recognition of a new government instituted by force, before consulting among themselves for the purpose of determining whether this government complies with the inter-American undertakings of the defense of the Continent, nor before carrying out an exchange of information as

---

Finally, almost two years later, with Martinez still in power, Costa Rica and El Salvador renounced the 1923 treaty and Costa Rica recognized the Martinez regime. Shortly thereafter the other three Central American states extended recognition through an agreement that the 1923 treaty would continue to bind them, but would not bind either Costa Rica or El Salvador. The United States accorded recognition one day after the Central American states. Department of State, Bureau of Public Affairs, Historical Office, *U.S. Policy toward Latin America: Recognition and Non-recognition of Governments and Interruptions in Diplomatic Relations, 1933–1974* (June 1975), pp. 1–5.

[60] Ibid., p. 12. Between 1934 and 1937, the United States confronted six extraconstitutional assumptions of power in Latin America: (1) Ecuador—October 1943 —Paez Government; (2) Paraguay—March 1936—Franco Government; (3) Bolivia —May 1936—Toro Government; (4) Bolivia—July 1937—Busch Government; 5) Paraguay—August 1937—Paiva Government; and (6) Ecuador—November 1937—Enriquez Government. In each coup, the military either assumed power itself or installed a man to head the new government. In each case, the United States granted formal recognition within a month, and contented itself with *pro forma* statements that the new government would honor all international obligations.

to the circumstances which have determined the establishment of the said government.[61]

With the advent of the war, and the establishment of the inter-
American committee, the attitude of the new regime toward the war,
and specifically toward the Axis powers, became of prime importance
in the recognition decision.[62]

The influence of the war issue on the U.S. recognition decision
is illustrated in the assumption of power in Argentina by General
Edelmiro Farrell in February 1944. Upon taking control, the Farrell
government appointed a pro-Axis general as the head of press and
information, granted contracts to German firms for the construction
of barracks, and censored U.S. films. The United States reacted
strongly to these moves, stating that it had "reason to believe that
groups not in sympathy with the declared Argentine policy of join-
ing the defense of the Hemisphere were active" in the assumption
of power by Farrell.[63] The U.S. ambassador recommended a "minimum
action program" as a precondition to recognition to include "liquida-
tion of all Axis organizations and propaganda media, control of prin-

---

[61] Department of State, *Problem of Recognition in American Foreign Policy*, p. 69.
For example, the United States withheld recognition when Major Gualberto
Villarroel assumed power in Bolivia in December 1943. On the day of the coup,
the U.S. ambassador recommended that recognition not be granted until the
government deported certain Nazis and Japanese. Secretary Hull on December
22 told the press that the attitude of the Villarroel government toward the war
effort was of first importance and the United States was concerned whether outside influence unfriendly to the Allied cause played any part in the assumption of
power by Villarroel.
Secretary Hull went further on January 24 and accused the Villarroel government of links to subversive elements hostile to the Allied cause. According to
Hull, the Bolivian coup was "but one act committed by a general subversive
movement having for its purpose steadily expanding activities on the continent."
Nineteen Latin American states refused to recognize the Villarroel government
on the same grounds. The "Axis taint" precluded recognition. In May, Villarroel
offered to trade the deportation of Axis nationals for United States recognition.
The United States refused the offer.
However, the Bolivian cabinet voted to detain and expel Axis nationals any-
way because it wished to identify itself with the Allied war effort. Based on
this and other actions friendly to the Allied cause, and after extensive contact
between American and Bolivian officials, the United States finally extended
recognition on June 23. Department of State, *U.S. Policy toward Latin America*,
pp. 14–18.
[62] Department of State, *Problem of Recognition in American Foreign Policy*,
p. 69.
[63] On April 4, the Argentine chargé d'affaires in Mexico City signed the final
act of the Inter-American Conference which called for freedom of the press and
protection of individual liberties. On April 9, the United States and twenty other
Western Hemisphere states agreed to resume relations. Department of State,
U.S. Policy toward Latin America, p. 24.

cipal Nazi business firms, and internment of Axis diplomats."[64] Non-recognition continued for a year until Argentina on March 27, 1945, declared war on the Axis states and pledged adherence to the acts of the Mexico City conference.[65]

In contrast to the lengthy delay where Axis sympathy was suspected, the United States promptly granted recognition to new regimes in Ecuador in June 1944 and Guatemala in November 1944. The United States did wait until elections were held in the case of Guatemala, but since elections were held only two weeks after the coup, the delay was not substantial.[66]

Other Parts of the World. Outside the Western Hemisphere, President Roosevelt generally adhered to the principle of nonintervention.[67] The President refused to grant recognition in the Spanish Civil War until all effective resistance to the national regime had ended. In the grant of recognition to the Franco government, President Roosevelt followed the traditional policy of recognizing a new government solely on the basis of its de facto existence.[68]

However, the question of recognition did not arise in areas outside Latin America often enough to result in the development of a consistently applied policy. Africa, which was to become a fertile ground for military coups in the 1960s, was still under colonial con-

---

[64] Ibid.

[65] Ibid.

[66] On June 7, 1943, following the resignation of President Arturo Rawson of Argentina, General Pedro P. Ramirez assumed the presidency and command of the armed forces. The United States accorded recognition four days later after receiving assurances that the new regime would support the war effort. The tenor of the United States position is reflected in a statement made to the Argentine Foreign Ministry upon the grant of recognition: "[The United States views] with satisfaction the public declarations of the new Argentine Government affirming a policy of friendship and loyal cooperation with the nations of America in accordance with the agreements in force, and that this policy will be implemented by acts. This assurance is especially welcome in view of the fact that these agreements were designed to protect the safety of all American nations which now is gravely threatened by the lawless aggressors." Department of State, *U.S. Policy toward Latin America*, p. 14.

[67] The statement of Secretary Hull in a letter to Representative Tinkham on May 16, 1936, was frequently referred to by officers of the Department of State to explain the prerequisites to recognition of new governments: "It is the rule of the United States 'to defer recognition of another executive in its place until it shall appear that it is in possession of the machinery of the state, administering government with the assent of the people thereof and without substantial resistance to its authority, and that it is in a position to fulfill all the international obligations and responsibilities incumbent upon a sovereign state under treaties and international law.' " Whiteman, *Digest of International Law*, vol 2, p. 71.

[68] Department of State, *Problem of Recognition in American Foreign Policy*, p. 70.

trol. Liberia was an exception, and the United States accorded recognition to the administration of President Edwin Barclay in June 1935. Europe of course did not spawn many coups d'etat or revolutions during this time, although the annexation of sovereign states by the Axis powers did raise recognition problems, both at the time of conquest and at the time of liberation and the formation of new governments. The Near East and South Asia as well as the Far East were still largely under colonial control, or were relatively stable during the Roosevelt years.

The Recognition Policy of Harry Truman

Latin America. A move to codify inter-American recognition practice was made in 1945 when Guatemala presented a draft resolution to the Inter-American Conference in Mexico City. The resolution, which did not enjoy U.S. support, provided that American nations refrain from granting recognition to antidemocratic regimes that might establish themselves in any state in the hemisphere. The Guatemalan resolution was defeated. However, two resolutions on the issue were adopted. The first stated that the right of maintaining, suspending, or renewing diplomatic relations should not be exercised as a means of obtaining unjustified advantages under international law. The second resolution provided that the establishment or maintenance of diplomatic relations with a government did not imply any judgment upon the domestic policies of that government.[69]

In the Truman years, nineteen changes of government in Latin America were achieved through extraconstitutional means. Almost all the changes were military-inspired, and in over half (ten of nineteen) the United States delayed recognition. This reflected a policy decision made within the Department of State to proceed cautiously in recognizing military governments.[70]

Dean Acheson characterized the recognition policy toward changes of government in Latin American in a 1949 speech to the Pan American Society:

> Our policy with respect to recognizing new governments in Latin America is not inconsistent with our encouragement of democracy. We maintain diplomatic relations with other countries primarily because we are all on the same planet and must do business with each other. . . . When a freely elected government is overthrown and a new and perhaps

---

[69] Ibid., pp. 87–88.
[70] Department of State, *U.S. Policy toward Latin America*, pp. 27–54.

militaristic government takes over, we do not need to recognize the new government automatically and immediately. We can wait to see if it really controls its territory and intends to live up to its international commitments. We can consult with other governments, as we have often done. But if and when we do recognize a government under these circumstances, our act of recognition need not be taken to imply approval of it or its policy.[71]

This policy resulted in ultimate recognition of most military governments after a short delay to determine if the regime controlled the territory of the state and was willing to honor its international obligations. Delay also resulted from the practice of consulting with other American states. In practice, as George Kennan aptly noted, recognition was accorded after an interval neither so short as to be undignified nor so long as to make recognition a source of conflict between the United States and the new governments.[72]

In the majority of instances the United States accorded recognition within a month after it satisfied itself that the usual criteria had been fulfilled. The following statement prepared for Secretary Acheson for use regarding the June 1951 military coup d'etat in Bolivia is representative:

> From appearances to date the Junta has met the criteria which the U.S. has applied in other recent cases involving the recognition of Latin American governments which have come to power through irregular procedures. It has established its authority over Bolivian territory, with the substantial acquiescence of its people, it has declared its intent to honor Bolivian international obligations, and its assumption of power has not been due to any external influences.[73]

In certain cases when the United States was displeased, especially where a constitutional government was overthrown by the military, as in Venezuela in November 1948, recognition was delayed for a period of months. This was sometimes accompanied by United States interest in a promise to return to constitutional government.[74]

---

[71] Ibid., p. 48.

[72] Ibid., p. 42.

[73] Ibid., p. 51.

[74] For example, recognition was delayed for several months in response to the January 11, 1946, assumption of power in Haiti by the military. The United States acted cautiously because it did not wish to encourage the establishment of military regimes that promised to observe democratic practices to gain recognition but then ignored their promises after recognition was granted. Department of State, *U.S. Policy toward Latin America*, pp. 45–46.

However, the United States was hesitant to utilize recognition as a club to secure the promise of elections. For example, in the February 1949 forced resignation of President Juan Natalicio Gonzalez of Paraguay, the American chargé recommended that recognition not be granted and that relations be suspended until the new government complied with its promise to hold elections. The Department of State rejected this approach, doubting that the suspension of relations, and presumably the withholding of recognition, would effectively encourage democratic processes or increase stability.[75]

Other Parts of the World. Like the Roosevelt administration, the Truman administration did not confront, at least in the traditional sense, enough extraconstitutional changes of government outside Latin America to develop a policy. The "minimal" recognition criteria were applied in a routine fashion, as this response to a coup d'etat in Syria in 1949 reflects:

> The Legation has been instructed to inform the Ministry that the United States Government has noted with satisfaction the public assurances which His Excellency the Prime Minister, Colonel Husni Zaim, has made affirming the intention of the new Syrian Government to discharge Syria's obligations arising out of all treaties and international agreements entered into by previous Syrian Governments, as well as its attachment to democratic principles and its intention to hold new elections at an early date.
>
> The Legation avails itself of this opportunity to renew to the Ministry the assurances of its highest consideration.[76]

---

[75] A similar hesitance is found in the response of Secretary Acheson to another coup in Paraguay in 1949, where he felt that to withhold recognition until after elections occurred "might be interpreted as an endorsement of the quality of these elections."

This interpretation, the secretary felt, would be particularly damaging since it would lend support to the erroneous but widely held belief that recognition implied approval of a new regime. To rebut this misconception, the secretary stressed on numerous occasions, such as the takeover by Arnulfo Arias in Panama in December 1949, that recognition did not constitute "approval of the manner in which the present government came into power." Department of State, *U.S. Policy toward Latin America*, pp. 46–47.

[76] Whiteman, *Digest of International Law*, vol. 2, p. 455. Similarly, when another government was formed in Syria on August 14, 1949, it was promptly recognized on the same criteria: "The United States Government relies upon the assurances given to it by the Syrian Government that Syria intends to honor its international obligations, and trusts that the friendly relations between our two nations will be continued. The promulgation on September 11, 1949, of a new electoral law reflecting the Syrian Government's intention to hold elections and form a constitutional government has also been noted." (Ibid., p. 455.)

However, the Truman administration faced difficult recognition decisions in two separate instances outside Latin America: (1) the assumption of power by Mao Tse-tung in China, and (2) the liberation of states in Central Europe from Axis control.

In perhaps the most celebrated instance on nonrecognition in modern times, the United States withheld recognition from the new government of the People's Republic of China, which was proclaimed in Peking on September 21, 1949. The establishment of a government headed by Mao Tse-tung followed the crossing of the Yangtze River by Communist troops, and the evacuation of Nanking by the government of the Republic of China. The government of the Republic of China moved to Canton, then to Chungking, and finally to Taipei in December 1949.

President Truman and the Department of State refused recognition to the new government and continued recognition of the Chiang Kai-shek government on several grounds. First, the Mao government was not in control of the entire land mass of China, and a rival government already recognized by the United States continued to function. Second, the new Communist government did not represent the will of the Chinese people. Third, the Communist government was not willing to honor all its international obligations. Fourth, as a sovereign state the United States was free to withhold recognition rather than accord recognition to a government that fomented revolution and hatred of the United States.[77] Nonrecognition continued for the duration of the Truman presidency.

Communist activity also presented President Truman with recognition problems in another area of the world, the sovereign states that had been conquered and occupied by the Axis powers during World War II. In February 1945 at the Yalta conference, the United States, Great Britain, and the Soviet Union in a unanimous "Declaration on Liberated Europe" agreed that the three governments would assist the liberated states "to form interim governmental authorities broadly representative of all democratic elements in the population and pledged to the earliest possible establishment through free elections of governments responsive to the will of the people."[78] In certain cases, such as Albania, major problems arose and recognition was not accorded.[79] However, in other instances elections were held, a new

---

[77] Ibid., pp. 90–110.

[78] Ibid., p. 408.

[79] Pursuant to the principles established at Yalta, the United States, through a diplomatic note of November 12, 1945, responded to a request for recognition from the new Albanian government and indicated its willingness to recognize the government of Albania provided that assurances were given that free elections

government was formed, and recognition was promptly accorded, as occurred in Poland.[80]

The Recognition Policy of Dwight Eisenhower

Latin America. Recognition policy toward Latin America under Eisenhower was dominated by two considerations: (1) the new regime should be in effective control of the state; and (2) the new regime should be anti-Communist. If both factors were met, recognition was promptly extended, even though in some instances an elected president might be replaced by a right-wing military junta that repressed human rights or violated civil liberties. While the United States still inquired whether the new regime was willing to honor its international obligations, this was, in most cases, merely *pro forma*. Elections were seldom mentioned when the United States extended recognition, and rarely was a promise to hold elections, legislative or presidential, advanced as a condition to recognition.

The Eisenhower administration faced nineteen instances in Latin America where the question of recognition arose. In only two cases was recognition delayed, and then for only six weeks. In most situations, a non-Communist bent plus effective control was enough to gain recognition.[81]

A number of the military regimes that were accorded quick recognition because of their anti-Communist beliefs did promise to hold free elections, apparently on their own initiative.[82] While the

---

would be held and that the treaties and agreements in effect between the United States and Albania on April 7, 1939, remained in effect. Assurances were given with respect to democratic elections but problems developed over certain bilateral treaties, and the government of Albania refused to accede to the treaties until certain "corrections" had been made. (Whiteman, *Digest of International Law*, vol. 1, pp. 322–325.) These treaties were never "corrected" and to the present, the United States does not recognize the government of Albania.

[80] Whiteman, *Digest of International Law*, vol. 2, pp. 410–412.

[81] On January 1, 1959, following years of revolutionary activity by Fidel Castro, President Batista fled Cuba. On the evening of January 1, Fidel Castro proclaimed Manuel Urrutialleo to be provisional president. The United States extended recognition on January 7 in a formal diplomatic note. Two years later, in January 1961, President Eisenhower broke diplomatic and consular relations with the government of Cuba. Nonetheless, recognition of the Fidel Castro regime continued. Ibid., pp. 268–270.

[82] For example, the United States granted recognition to a military junta six days after it overthrew the elected president of Honduras, Julio Lozano Diaz, on October 21, 1956. The United States accorded recognition because the junta was considered friendly to the United States and was anti-Communist, and in addition, had announced its willingness to fulfill its international obligations, and restore constitutional rule through elections. Department of State, *U.S. Policy toward Latin America*, pp. 58–59.

United States was undoubtedly glad to receive such assurances (Haiti, 1956; Honduras, 1956; Venezuela, 1958), there is no evidence that it demanded such promises as a condition to recognition.

Indeed, on several occasions the Department of State refused to rely on a promise to return to constitutional government as a condition to the grant of recognition. For example, in the June, 1957 takeover by General Antono Kebreau in Haiti, the American ambassador requested that recognition be deferred until the intentions of the new regime toward elections became clear. The Department of State rejected this suggestion, arguing that conditioning the grant of recognition on the holding of elections constituted intervention in the domestic affairs of Haiti.[83]

Other Parts of the World. Eisenhower, like Roosevelt and Truman before him, did not confront many recognition decisions outside Latin America. The significant cases included Vietnam (1953), Tunisia (1957), Iraq (1958), Burma (1958), Pakistan (1958), Korea (1960), Laos (1960), Turkey (1960), and the continuing problem of the refusal to recognize the People's Republic of China.

The July 14, 1958, coup in Iraq is representative of the Eisenhower policy. Here the military overthrew the monarchy of Iraq and almost immediately announced that it would honor all its international obligations, including those relating to petroleum. On July 30, Secretary of State Dulles recommended to President Eisenhower that the United States recognize the new government of Iraq.

I believe that we should shortly recognize the new government in Iraq. Although we deplore the brutality which characterized its seizure of power, the new regime has quickly restored order, is in full control of the country and apparently faces no organized opposition. The Foreign Minister and other officials have repeatedly said that Iraq wishes to continue close friendly relations as well as economic cooperation, particularly in oil matters, with the United States and other Western powers. These assertions have been accompanied by public assurances that the new government would fulfill Iraq's international treaty obligations.[84]

---

[83] Ibid., pp. 65–66.

[84] Whiteman, *Digest of International Law*, vol. 2, pp. 450–451. The recommendation continued: "The question of recognition of the Iraqi Republic has been discussed with representatives of the Muslim Baghdad Pact countries, Iran, Turkey and Pakistan, who have indicated their understanding of the advisability of our recognizing the new Iraqi Government without undue delay so as to be in the best position to protect United States interests in Iraq and to exert constructive

United States recognition policy throughout the 1950s was distorted somewhat by the continued nonrecognition of the People's Republic of China. While in the normal case the United States followed the de facto approach with anticommunism an additional criterion, State Department officials often defended the nonrecognition policy towards Communist China in sweeping, doctrinal terms, causing confusion and misstating general policy. For example, Secretary Dulles stated in an address in 1954:

> Let me first recall that diplomatic recognition is a voluntary act. One country has no right to demand recognition by another. Generally, it is useful that there should be diplomatic intercourse between those who exercise *de facto* governmental authority, and it is well established that recognition does not imply moral approval.
>
> President Monroe, in his famous message to Congress, denounced the expansionist and despotic system of Czarist Russia and its allies. But he said that it would nevertheless be our policy "to consider the government *de facto* as the legitimate government for us." This has indeed been the general United States policy, and I believe that it is a sound policy. However, where it does not serve our interests, we are free to vary from it.
>
> In relation to Communist China, we are forced to take account of the fact that the Chinese Communist regime has been consistently and viciously hostile to the United States.[85]

Summary

U.S. recognition policy from the time of Jefferson until 1960 was complex and changing. There was much confusion and disagreement over the proper role of recognition from one administration to another, and usually significant confusion and inconsistency within an administra-

---

influence upon the new regime. It is expected that the Baghdad Pact countries also will soon extend recognition. The Governments of Lebanon and Jordan have similarly expressed to us in private their appreciation of the considerations which argue for early recognition by the United States. Other Arab states, such as Saudi Arabia and Tunisia, have already extended recognition. We will wish to consult with other friendly nations, such as the NATO powers, but your authority is now sought for the United States to extend formal diplomatic recognition to the Republic of Iraq as soon as such action is deemed appropriate." The United States extended recognition on August 2, 1958 (ibid.).

[85] Department of State, "The Threat of a Red Asia," address by Secretary of State Dulles, *Bulletin*, vol. 30 (April 12, 1959), pp. 539–540.

tion. U.S. policy varied from a de facto policy of almost automatic recognition to the active use of recognition to achieve policy goals.

The changing nature of recognition policy and the inconsistent application of the policy continued into the Kennedy administration, to which we now turn.

2

U.S. RECOGNITION POLICY UNDER JOHN F. KENNEDY, 1961-1963

Latin America

President John F. Kennedy based his recognition policy toward Latin America on two deeply held views—his antipathy toward military dictatorships and his belief in the need for social, economic, and political progress through the Alliance for Progress. Kennedy's basic foreign policy, vividly reflected in his recognition policy toward Latin America, broke sharply with U.S. foreign policy under Eisenhower. In the 1950s the United States accepted de facto military regimes obtaining power through coup d'etat, and gave them military, economic, and humanitarian assistance. If the new regime was friendly and anti-Communist, it could count on a warm United States response. One historian has observed that "the operative premise seemed to be that dictators offered the surest defense against the threat of communism."[1]

Kennedy rejected the complacent acceptance of military regimes and strongly denounced militarism in Latin America. He believed that democratic, constitutional government was a precondition to the social and economic development Latin America so badly needed and therefore he premised his most ambitious Latin American programs on the development of strong, constitutional government.[2] Consequently, the Kennedy administration viewed military coups d'etat in Latin America with considerable distaste and sought a return to constitutional government in as short a period as possible. As one writer commented:

---

[1] E. Lieuwen, *Generals vs. Presidents—Neomilitarism in Latin America* (Praeger: New York, 1964), p. 114.

[2] Ibid., p. 115.

43

EXTRACONSTITUTIONAL CHANGES OF GOVERNMENT IN FOREIGN STATES DURING THE PRESIDENCY OF JOHN F. KENNEDY

Latin America

1. *El Salvador, January 1961.* Military coup led by Colonel Alberto Rivera overthrew Colonel Miguel Castillo.
2. *Ecuador, November 1961.* Jose Maria Velasco Ibarra under pressure resigned in favor of Vice President Carlos Julio Arosemena Monroy.
3. *Dominican Republic, January 1962.* Dictator Rafael Trujillo assassinated, but conspirators unable to seize power. In December, however, President Balaguer fled into asylum. After some turmoil, Council of State restored under Rafael Bonnelly.
4. *Argentina, March 1962.* Military coup removed President Arturo Frondizi.
5. *Peru, June 1962.* Manuel Prado removed by military coup.
6. *Guatemala, March 1963.* Military coup ousted President Miguel Ydigoras Fuentes in favor of Colonel Enrique Peralta Azurdia, the defense minister.
7. *Ecuador, July 1963.* Military junta took power, ousting President Arosemena.
8. *Dominican Republic, September 1963.* President Juan Bosch removed by the military.
9. *Honduras, October 1963.* The military, led by Colonel Oswaldo Lopez Arellano, removed President Ramon Villeda Morales.

Africa

10. *Togo, January 1963.* President Sylvanus Olympio killed in coup, power handed to President Grunitzky.
11. *Congo-Brazzaville, August 1963.* Abbe Youlou overthrown, army gave power to Massemba-Debat.
12. *Dahomey (Benin), October 1963.* Colonel Soglo seized power in a bloodless coup.

Far East

13. *South Korea, May 1961.* The military, led by Major General Chung Hee Park and Colonel Kim Chong P'il, overthrew government of Chang Myon.
14. *Burma, March 1962.* General Ne Win overthrew Premier U Nu and established military regime.

Near East and South Asia

15. *Syria, September 1961.* Rightist military officers withdrew Syria from United Arab Republic and returned the government to conservative rule.

16. *Yemen, September 1962.* Yemeni republicans overthrew Imam al-Badr, who had ruled for only a week following the death of his father, Imam Ahmad.
17. *Iraq, February 1963.* A Ba'th Party conspiracy with army assistance overthrew the pro-Communist Kassem government. The prime minister was executed.
18. *Syria, March 1963.* In cooperation with military elements, the leftist Ba'th Party assumed control.

Given the official desire of the United States for social and economic progress as well as political stability in the Americas, the possibility of a coup d'etat was considered anathema by most administration spokesmen. They felt, typically, that military usurpation of power would obfuscate the basic principles of the inter-American system and, further, that the legacy of interference was often a hardened anti-militaristic sentiment and disillusionment with the electoral process.[3]

During Kennedy's three-year term, seven coups occurred in Latin America; all seven were military-backed, and six of them deposed presidents who had been elected.[4] Recognition policy toward the military coups was in general quite stern, especially toward the assumption of power by the military in Peru in 1962 and in Honduras in 1963. In making the decision to recognize, Kennedy often bartered recognition for the reestablishment of constitutional government through elections. His success in achieving his objective was mixed.

Kennedy strayed from the path of democratic idealism on certain occasions and recognized military regimes even though their commitment to constitutional government was something less than complete, notably in Guatemala and Ecuador in 1963.

El Salvador, 1961. On January 25, 1961, the military in El Salvador overthrew a six-man ruling body which itself had assumed power by coup d'etat in October 1960. The coup did not greatly disturb the United States, since one anti-Castro military junta replaced another and the new junta promised a revised election law and a restoration of civil liberties.[5]

---

[3] Theodore Maher, "The Kennedy and Johnson Responses to Latin American Coups d'Etat," *World Affairs*, vol. 131, p. 185.

[4] This listing is somewhat arbitrary as the line between extraconstitutional and merely irregular changes of government was blurred during the Kennedy years. For one scholar's listing of coups d'etat under Presidents Kennedy and Johnson, see Appendix B. See also Lieuwen, *Generals vs. Presidents*, p. 5.

[5] Maher, "Kennedy and Johnson Responses," p. 186.

Nevertheless, Kennedy set the pattern for later U.S. responses to military coups in Latin America by emphasizing the return to constitutional government through free elections in the grant of recognition. In a press statement he stressed the importance of democratic government:

> I have a statement that we have today [February 15] recognized the Government of El Salvador. It has announced its determination to bring about free and democratic elections in that country, and it seeks solutions for the economic and social difficulties which that country has faced. These objectives are in consonance with our goal of a free and prosperous Latin America. Manifestoes of the Government and its agencies have indicated a clear determination to improve the standard of living of the people of that country, particularly those engaged in agriculture. We hope to be able to assist El Salvador in reaching these goals under the spirit of the Act of Bogota.[6]

Ecuador, 1961, and Dominican Republic, 1962. Arguably extraconstitutional changes of government occurred in Ecuador in 1961 and in the Dominican Republic in 1962.

Following rioting and civil disorder in Ecuador, Vice President Arosemena was proclaimed president unanimously by the Congress of Ecuador on November 7, 1961. President Velasco Ibarra took asylum in the Mexican embassy, stating that he had not resigned his post. The assumption of power was confirmed by the Council of State, although the Ecuadorean Congress never formally declared Velasco Ibarra out of office as required by the Ecuadorean constitution.[7] The United States took the position that no question of recognition arose because the assumption of power was constitutional.

On January 1, 1962, a seven-member Council of State seized power in the Dominican Republic. However, later in the month, Gen-

---

[6] "Press Conference of February 15, 1961," in *Public Papers of the Presidents of the United States: John F. Kennedy*, Washington, D.C., 1962, p. 92.

[7] Under Articles 87 and 88 of the Ecuadorean constitution, if a president legally ceased the function of his office by resignation, abandonment of post, or dismissal of Congress, the vice-president could assume the functions of the presidency. Also, under Article 91, when Velasco abandoned his post and took asylum he arguably gave up his title to the presidency. Although the Ecuadorean Congress did not formally declare Velasco out of office as the article provides, it did, by unanimous vote, designate Arosemena as successor under Article 87. In addition, the Council of States affirmed the succession of Arosemena and administered the oath of office, thereby officially indicating the council's acceptance of the abdication of Velasco and the assumption of power by Arosemena. The United States continued relations after Arosemena was sworn in as president on November 9.

eral Rodriquez Echavarria arrested members of the Council of State and assumed power. Kennedy responded with vigor to the military junta led by General Echavarria, removing the economic aid mission and refusing to recognize the junta. In an attempt to isolate the Echavarria regime, Kennedy did not complete a $45 million purchase of sugar from the Dominican Republic; he also considered a recall of the Inter-American Development Bank mission.[8] The policy proved successful and the junta was overthrown by a military counter-coup on January 18, which restored the Council of State to office under Rafael Bonnelly. Consequently, no question of recognition was considered to arise.

Argentina, 1962. The Argentina coup of March 1962 presented President Kennedy for the first time with the overthrow of a democratically elected, constitutional government. Despite misgivings, the United States concluded that the question of recognition did not arise, because President Arturo Frondizi was replaced by Senate President Jose Maria Guido.

Other states took similar action. Colombia announced that the transfer of power to Guido was constitutional and that it would continue relations with the government of Argentina. Peru delayed recognition, presumably to make sure that Guido was in firm control of the government. A number of Western European governments were under pressure to take action to continue relations with the new government of Argentina. In contrast, Costa Rica announced on March 30, 1962, that in accordance with its recently adopted policy it would not recognize the new government of Argentina. The government of Costa Rica had adopted the Betancourt Doctrine, which refused recognition to any government that attained power through extraconstitutional means.

On April 7, Bolivia announced that it was continuing relations with the government of Argentina. The British on April 10 acknowledged the note of Argentina. Holland and Germany, along with all of the Scandinavian countries, indicated that they would continue relations. Venezuela stated relatively early (April 5) that it would not recognize the new government of Argentina. Betancourt claimed that he had promised Frondizi in October 1960 not to maintain relations with governments not freely elected. Venezuela's position was one of "belligerent association" with the Argentine regime. Ecuador stated on April 11 that it would recognize the new government of Argentina shortly. Ecuador was in all probability delaying in order to have its

---

[8] Maher, "Kennedy and Johnson Responses," p. 187.

recognition timed about the same time as other states. Uruguay recognized the new government on May 22 in a note in reply to the Argentine note announcing Guido's assumption of the presidency. The note merely acknowledged receipt of the Argentine message. Uruguay was in a difficult position since further delay in recognition of its powerful neighbor would hurt its future relations.

The United States had attempted to prevent the coup by warning the Argentine armed forces that a military takeover would subvert the ideals of the Alliance for Progress and weaken constitutional government. The Argentine generals rejected this advice and seized power.

Although the United States considered cutting off aid and withholding recognition, it finally concluded that the form of constitutionality had been preserved and therefore no question of recognition arose.[9] The United States delayed for some time in reaching this decision, as observers felt that military support for Guido was not firm and he was not yet in effective control. In addition, one can hypothesize that early U.S. recognition would have hindered Guido's chances of dealing with the threat of Peronista disorders. The United States also apparently was worried that early recognition would be interpreted as an implicit signal for military intervention before the upcoming elections.

Peru, 1962. President Kennedy hardened his stance toward extraconstitutional changes of government in Latin America in the July 18, 1962, military takeover in Peru. The coup followed the June 10 election of Haya de la Torre. Upon learning of the change of government, President Kennedy suspended diplomatic relations, cut off economic aid, and stopped military assistance.[10] Involved in this cancellation of aid was $81 million of Alliance for Progress funds guaranteed by the United States and military aid which ran at about $5 million a year. President Kennedy announced his dismay at the setback to democracy. Ambassador Loeb returned to Washington, and all United States assistance to Peru, except for humanitarian aid, was halted.[11]

One commentator has characterized President Kennedy's response to the Peruvian coup as "the high point of his pique and impatience with military intervention."[12] The commentator continued:

> The Kennedy response to the Peruvian rebellion raised
> a fundamental question. Was the application of punitive

---

[9] Lieuwen, *Generals vs. Presidents*, p. 115.

[10] Ibid., p. 116.

[11] Maher, "Kennedy and Johnson Responses," p. 187.

[12] Ibid.

measures against the junta in consonance with the nature of the offense, especially in view of the administration's comparatively cavalier attitude toward the Argentine upheaval three and one-half months earlier? Kennedy's actions and reproof were nevertheless consistent with his policy pronouncements. The provocation was great. Peru had had an honest, carefully safeguarded presidential election in 1962. The military leaders annulled it, arrested the president, and seized power for themselves. The administration's lightning move to impose what amounts to diplomatic, economic, and military sanctions symbolized new determination by the United States to have its Latin American neighbors live up to the principles of the inter-American system.[13]

Peru serves as the best example of the use of recognition and financial aid as bargaining levers to obtain a promise to return to constitutional government through free elections. The Kennedy response to the Peruvian coup was designed to establish a principle and "serve notice on other plotters that the United States had decided to draw a line when anti-democratic circumstances develop."[14]

The stern U.S. response put American policy makers in a difficult position. The Peruvian military had been friendly to the United States, cooperated in a number of international and regional activities, and was a strong bulwark against disorders from the left. On the other hand, achievement of the objectives of the Alliance for Progress in Peru, and to some extent in the rest of the hemisphere, would depend upon the restoration of a democratic system in Peru.[15]

There were several dangers to the United States in its strong negative position. It might be forced to back down, or become isolated in the hemisphere, as a result of the nonrecognition stance. The stand might alienate permanently the Peruvian military and weaken or destroy the democratic political processes in Peru. Nonetheless, President Kennedy took a hardline position and demanded, in return for recognition and the resumption of aid: (1) the release of the imprisoned former president; (2) a promise of free, constitutional elections by June 13, 1963; (3) a restoration of civil liberties; and (4) an

---

[13] Ibid., p. 188.

[14] Ibid., p. 189.

[15] Venezuela proposed a meeting of foreign ministers of the Organization of American States to consider this problem of military coups and of the Peruvian coup in particular. The United States, while sympathetic to the proposal, opposed it because of the effect it would have on the Peruvian military junta. In an attempt at compromise, the United States submitted a middle-of-the-road resolution on the issue to the Meeting of Foreign Ministers. However, the resolution did not satisfy either Venezuela or Peru and went down to defeat.

increase in the number of civilians in the interim government. The U.S. suspension of aid and refusal of recognition caused unease in Peru, and the junta requested a meeting with American embassy officials. However, in the meeting the junta showed no real inclination to return to civilian control of the government.

Eventually, when other states in the hemisphere recognized the junta, the United States was forced to follow suit to avoid becoming isolated. To make the U.S. action less embarrassing, the junta promised to hold elections within a reasonable time; however, it did not set a date.

Recognition was granted on August 17. In the public announcement that went with the recognition grant, the United States pointed out that the action was based on the junta's effective control of the government and the country and its pledge to fulfill Peru's international obligations. The United States indicated that it attached significance to the junta's guarantee to respect the results of free elections and to restore civil liberties. The announcement also stated that the United States welcomed the open-door policy announced before the Council of the OAS on August 8, which would permit international representatives of stature and responsibility to observe the carrying out of the electoral process.[16]

The United States had been under strong pressure to recognize the junta. Edwin Lieuwen commented:

> Thus, when the major Latin American and European nations, as well, recognized the junta—Argentina was the first to extend recognition—Kennedy's policy of international ostracism of the new Peruvian regime broke down. With almost no diplomatic support, except for several of the smaller Latin American nations, under pressure from the United States business interests in Peru and from the Peruvian populace (two-thirds of whom had supported presidential candidates other than Haya de la Torre), the United States on August 17 recognized Peru and restored economic aid and, a short time later, resumed military assistance. As a face-saving condition for recognition and aid, Washington did succeed in getting a promise from the junta to hold elections within a reasonable length of time, and, in the interim, to work for the economic and social progress of the Peruvian people.[17]

Military leaders in Latin America interpreted the Washington response to the Peruvian coup as "a green light . . . to right situations

---

[16] U.S. Department of State, *Bulletin*, vol. 47 (1962), p. 348.

[17] Lieuwen, *Generals vs. Presidents*, p. 116.

of civilian misrule," and four coups occurred in 1963 which followed the pattern established by Peru and Argentina:

> The formula for dealing with protests from Washington has been provided: Rationalize the coups by charges of Communist infiltration and gross misgovernment; follow this by promises to hold elections and restore constitutional processes within a "reasonable" length of time. This was the technique used by the juntas in Guatemala, Ecuador, the Dominican Republic, and Honduras. It worked in the first two countries; in the latter two, the officers ran into serious, though only temporary, difficulties.[18]

Guatemala, 1963. The pressures on the United States to compromise its principles of democratic idealism were even greater in the case of the military takeover in Guatemala in March 1963. President Ydigoras Fuentes, according to some, had presided over five years of graft and provided thoroughly inept and nonprogressive rule. When he was overthrown by Colonel Enrique Peralta Azurdia, the pressure to recognize the junta quickly was enhanced by the United States fear that Juan Arevalo, a bitter enemy of the United States, would be elected president if elections were held.[19]

By April 9, the new government had drafted a law establishing a charter of government that included civil liberties guarantees and a commitment to hold elections in the shortest possible time, not to exceed two years. There was some diffusion of governmental power among civilian as well as military elements and a commitment to honor international obligations. This was apparently adequate for the United States,[20] which granted recognition to the new regime on April 15. The recognition statement noted:

> The United States recognizes the new government of Guatemala. This action was taken after the United States

---

[18] Ibid., p. 117.

[19] Ibid. In this instance, as in the other situations in which the question of recognition arose, there was substantial interplay between the various governments considering the problem. As expected, the governments of Venezuela, Costa Rica and the Dominican Republic expressed the view that they would not recognize any government that was the result of an overthrow of a democratically elected government. Of the countries contiguous to Guatemala, and therefore important in the recognition decision of other countries, Honduras, El Salvador, and Nicaragua all agreed that early recognition would be the best course of action, and would support Central American stability. All recognized the new regime on April 8.

[20] However, on April 10 the Peralta regime broadcast a decree that did not include any commitment for elections, and at the same time established, in a separate decree, military courts to try a wide range of offenses under a new "law for defense of democracy" which provided for very harsh penalties.

ascertained that the new government was in full control and pledged to respect Guatemala's international obligations. This follows consultation with other governments in the hemisphere.[21]

In the official text, the United States cited Peralta's statement that there would be an effort to hold elections within two years.

There was a sharp contrast in the U.S. response to the Peruvian coup in 1962 and the U.S. response to the 1963 Guatemalan coup:

> In marked contrast to the swift and specific denunciation of the Peruvian armed forces was the Kennedy reaction to the Guatemalan and Ecuadorean military coups d'etat of March 31 and July 11, 1963. The administration reverted to enunciation of vague statements regarding the distasteful and counter-productive ramifications of military intrusion. The failure of the United States to go on record as deploring the changes of government indicates that President Kennedy, in this instance at least, followed an eclectic approach conditioned and shaped by the circumstances of the particular situation. Inevitably, the question arose as to whether the United States had a uniform policy regarding governments that took power by force. President Kennedy stated that there was no consistent position ". . . because the circumstances are sometimes inconsistent." In a similar vein, Secretary Rusk indicated that it was difficult to make a general statement about policy toward the military coup "that would apply in theoretical exactitude" to all of the countries with which the United States has relations. Thus, on the basis of government testimony and action, the formulation of a program was conditioned not only by a philosophical posture but by the often conflicting circumstances of national interest and inter-American obligations.[22] [Footnotes omitted.]

Brazil recognized the Guatemalan government on April 19 and Argentina recognized on April 22. Uruguay recognized on May 17.

Ecuador, 1963. The United States was also unhappy with President Arosemena of Ecuador because of his flirtation with Communist interests and his failure to sever relations with Cuba, in addition to his general ineptness and serious drinking problem.[23] Consequently, when a military takeover occurred in July 1963, recognition was accorded

---

[21] U.S. Department of State, *Press Release*, April 15, 1963.

[22] Maher, "Kennedy and Johnson Responses," p. 191.

[23] Lieuwen, *Generals vs. Presidents*, p. 118.

the new regime in less than three weeks in return for a promise that elections would be held in a reasonable time.

There were a number of crosscurrents and conflicting regional interests involved that affected the U.S. position. First among these was the border dispute between Ecuador and Peru which had been addressed in the Rio Protocol. Peru took the position that recognition should be conditioned on Ecuadorean acceptance of all international obligations. Peru's concern arose from the equivocal wording about international obligations contained in the note that the Ecuadorean junta had sent to various nations.

On July 24, Great Britain, Nationalist China, and Lebanon recognized the military government of Ecuador. In contrast, Ecuador recalled its ambassadors to Venezuela, Costa Rica, and Honduras due to the actions of these states in officially suspending relations.

Chile during this period was increasingly recognizing governments without regard to approval or disapproval of the regime, on the theory that approval or disapproval constituted intervention in internal affairs. Brazil took the same position as it did in the case of Guatemala and Peru—that the form of government was an internal matter—and once the normal requirements were met Brazil was prepared to recognize. It would not, however, be the first to extend recognition, nor the last. Argentina agreed with this approach. Bolivia recognized on August 2. By August 9, twenty-two countries had recognized the regime. Peru waited until September 9 to recognize. On July 31, the United States officially recognized the new regime in Ecuador.[24]

The Ecuadorean coup marks a departure from President Kennedy's pursuit of democratic, constitutional government in Latin America, a departure brought about by other pressing political interests. One writer characterized the U.S. position on the Ecuadorean coup as a complete sacrifice of democratic principles made "to get rid of a constitutional government it considered inimical to its interests."[25]

Dominican Republic, 1963. On September 26, 1963, the military overthrew Juan Bosch, the elected president of the Dominican Republic. The United States was unhappy with the change of government. On October 4, Secretary of State Rusk issued a statement strongly criticizing the coup,[26] adding that under existing circumstances no oppor-

---

[24] U.S. Department of State, *Press Release*, July 31, 1963.

[25] Lieuwen, *Generals vs. Presidents*, p. 118.

[26] The text of the statement: "We view the recent military coups in the Dominican Republic and Honduras with the utmost gravity. The establishment and maintenance of representative constitutional government is an essential element in the

tunity existed for a normalization of diplomatic relations. The secretary further ordered all economic and military aid stopped, and he began the reassignment of personnel involved in these activities. Latin American states adopted the same approach. As of October 19, no Latin American government had recognized the new Dominican triumvirate except for the military government of Honduras, itself recently installed by a coup.

President Kennedy was queried on the coup in a press conference on November 14. He indicated that it was a question for the entire hemisphere, noting that the OAS, by a vote of eighteen to one, had agreed to a meeting on the problem of military coups. He further stated that the United States had inquired what steps each of the two countries (Dominican Republic and Honduras) was prepared to take to return to constitutional government, a move the United States strongly urged. The question was then posed whether the United States would accept the same conditions for recognition in the Dominican Republic as it had in the case of the junta in Peru—elections in one year, for example. The president responded:

> Well, I think it would be unwise to attempt to negotiate this out here, but we did recognize the junta in Peru on the assurances that they would hold elections. They did hold them and the result was very fair. So it shows that it can be done. That is what we would like to see done in these countries.[27]

Informal conversations were held in Santo Domingo with officials of the new regime during November with a view to making firm plans to return to constitutional government within a reasonable period.

Progress was made toward recognition when the regime gave public assurances that it would respect civil liberties, allow freedom of action for political parties, and guarantee the fulfillment of international obligations. A decree was issued on November 26 setting forth the schedule for five elections, the first to be held between September 1 and November 30 of the next year for minor local officials. This would serve as a voter census. Municipal elections would follow on January 15, 1965, a constituent assembly election on March 1, 1965,

Alliance for Progress. Stable and effective government, responsive to the popular will, is the critical factor in the attainment of social and economic progress.

"Under existing conditions in the Dominican Republic and Honduras there is no opportunity for effective collaboration by the United States under the Alliance for Progress or for normalization of diplomatic relations. Accordingly, we have stopped all economic and military aid to these countries and have commenced orderly reassignment of the personnel involved." U.S. Department of State, *Bulletin*, vol. 45 (1963), p. 624.

[27] *Public Papers of the Presidents: John F. Kennedy*, p. 851.

and congressional elections on June 24, 1965. Presidential elections were scheduled for July 15, 1965, and the elected government would assume office on August 16, 1965.

The United States granted recognition on December 14, 1963. The Department of State gave a number of reasons for withholding recognition for a period of two-and-one-half months. According to the department the prime objective had been a return at the earliest possible date to constitutionally elected government. Other reasons were to weaken like-minded plotters in other parts of the hemisphere, to minimize violence and opportunities for extreme leftists to expand their strength, and to secure the fullest possible respect for civil liberties and non-Communist party activity pending a new election.[28]

The United States viewed the policy of nonrecognition as partially successful since it achieved the issuance of the decree setting up an election timetable. Recognition was granted when it became clear that prospects of gaining additional concessions were virtually nil and further delay would be counterproductive.

There were other reasons for the grant of recognition. U.S. ability to influence Dominican Republic developments would have decreased if the United States continued to withhold recognition since high world sugar prices and lack of general Dominican popular reaction against the new regime furnished clear evidence that the regime did not need U.S. recognition to survive. Recognition also would enable the United States to help the Dominicans stop possible Cuban arms shipments and strengthen the regime's position in suppressing disorders that could be used as a pretext by civilian and military elements to suppress political activity or to seize the government and cancel the election schedule. Finally, a number of hemisphere governments favored early recognition and withheld it only in deference to the U.S. initiative.

Honduras, 1963. The United States pursued a nonrecognition policy in the Honduran coup in October 1963, when the military, led by Colonel Lopez Arellano, overthrew President Villeda Morales. The United States took strong measures against the coup. On October 4, Secretary Rusk released a statement terminating all economic and military aid and indicating that there would be no opportunity for normalization of diplomatic relations under the existing circumstances.[29] The chiefs of U.S. army and air force missions in Honduras were transferred, and the State Department ordered the restationing

---

[28] U.S. Department of State, *Press Release*, December 14, 1963.

[29] U.S. Department of State, *Press Release*, October 4, 1963.

of the AID (Agency for International Development) director and other principal AID officials and terminated the employment of local employees of AID. The department also attempted to delay or stop financial assistance to Honduras from U.S. funds in international institutions. President Kennedy spoke out strongly against the Honduran coup.

The deposed president, Villeda Morales, asked the United States to intervene militarily against his own military forces.[30] President Kennedy emphatically ruled out military action: "[The] idea that we ought to send United States Marines into Honduras . . . is a very serious mistake. That is not the way . . . for democracy to flourish."[31]

The primary U.S. objective in withholding recognition was an orderly return to popularly elected government without the civil strife that might open the way for Cuban involvement. Central to U.S. policy was the need to delay Salvadorian, Nicaraguan, Costa Rican, and Panamanian recognition, efforts which if successful would constitute a major pressure for a return to constitutional rule.

As of October 18, Guatemala was the only American state to recognize the new government.[32] Elsewhere, only Spain, Lebanon, the Vatican, and the Republic of China had recognized the new government.

Although the shooting had stopped in Honduras, the political outcome of the post-coup situation was not stabilized. The new government was attempting to return to constitutional rule and was communicating with moderate opponents. The State Department viewed this as a positive step and one that would lead to a constitutional solution if the pressures on the regime could be maintained.

President Kennedy did not live to see the results of his policy towards the Honduran coup. Ironically, a breakthrough occurred on November 22, 1963, the day the President was assassinated. On that day a law was issued by the junta creating an electoral commission representing major parties and civil leaders. It called for preparation of a new electoral law by March 1, 1964, and revision of voter registrations by January 1, 1965. Constituent Assembly elections would be held February 15, 1965, and the assembly would be installed on

---

30 Maher, "Kennedy and Johnson Responses," p. 192.

31 *Public Papers of the Presidents: John F. Kennedy*, p. 771, cited in Maher, "Kennedy and Johnson Responses," p. 192.

32 Guatemalan recognition was regarded as insignificant since Guatemala was not a signatory of the five presidents' statement of September 30; it was also a military regime still operating without a constitution. The United States was still opposed to recognition of the new regime on October 12 and continued to lead the movement to withhold recognition. Despite some difficulties, El Salvador and Nicaragua continued to withhold recognition.

March 16, 1965, at which time it would receive the supreme power of the government. The electoral commission was sworn in on December 2 and began to hold meetings. In addition, the new regime gave public assurances on civil liberties, freedom of action for political parties and the fulfillment of international obligations. As a result of these actions, the United States moved to recognize, finally doing so on December 14.[33]

Four days before his death, President Kennedy had restated his belief in constitutional democracy and his unswerving determination to achieve such government in the Western Hemisphere:

> Political democracy and stability . . . is at the core of our hopes for the future.
>
> There can be no progress if people have no faith in tomorrow. That faith is undermined when men seek the reins of power, ignoring the restraints of constitutional procedures. They may even do so out of a sincere desire to benefit their own country. But democratic government demands that those in opposition accept the defeats of today and work toward remedying them within the machinery of peaceful change. Otherwise, in return for momentary satisfaction we tear apart the fabric and the hope of lasting democracy.
>
> Whatever may be the case in other parts of the world, this is a hemisphere of free men capable of self-government. It is in accordance with this belief that the United States will continue to support the efforts of those seeking to establish and maintain constitutional democracy.[34]

Although the President did not specifically refer to recognition, it is evident that he regarded it as one of the tools to be used to advance the cause of constitutional government. While his recognition practice was not totally consistent, and while political factors outweighed the advancement of constitutional government in particular instances, Kennedy followed the constitutional view in Latin America more closely than any President since Wilson.

Assessing the relative effectiveness of the U.S. response to coups d'etat in Latin America during the presidency of John F. Kennedy is, in the words of one historian, "a slippery process."[35] Where the United States pressed hard for assurances of a return to constitutional

---

[33] Argentina withheld recognition until the eve of United States action and granted recognition on December 11.

[34] *Public Papers of the Presidents: John F. Kennedy,* cited in Lieuwen, *Generals vs. Presidents,* p. 120.

[35] Maher, "Kennedy and Johnson Responses," p. 197.

government, some favorable results were achieved; for example, in Honduras in 1963. However, it is impossible to separate the concessions gained by withholding recognition from the concessions achieved by other action taken by the United States in response to coups. A variety of such actions occurred in each case where a policy objective was achieved. These included a general U.S. attitude of disapproval, strong public denouncements of the coup by U.S. officials, suspension of economic and military aid, and recall of the United States ambassador, portending the suspension of diplomatic relations. Such were the tools employed by President Kennedy to obtain his primary goal, a promise of free elections.

The Kennedy policy received considerable attention and criticism. James Reston found the U.S. approach in withholding recognition to be moralistic and nonpragmatic.[36] Arthur Krock criticized the timing of the retaliatory measures and proposed a "phased, conditioned-step technique . . . as a substitute for the abrupt . . . cessation of diplomatic relations and aid."[37]

In only two instances did the United States delay for more than one month in granting recognition. Sometimes this reflected rather prompt promises from the new government to hold elections. In other cases, it reflected a fundamental problem in the use of nonrecognition as a political tool: that if recognition is withheld for too long a period, the policy backfires, engendering hostility on the part of the new government and its people and creating substantial sentiment to resist U.S. pressure. Consequently, U.S. policy makers, when using recognition as a bargaining tool, were constantly mindful of the dangers of being boxed into a permanent state of nonrecognition. Further, recognition of the new government by other states often forces the United States to take action, as happened in Argentina in 1963. Table 1 sets out the time spans between Latin American coups, the U.S. recognition response, and the next election in the coup state.

In assessing the effectiveness of U.S. recognition policy under President Kennedy, it is also necessary to weigh an intangible—the hostility that the policy generated, both in the United States and in Latin America. The United States paid a substantial price for the assurances that it received in return for recognition and the resumption of military and economic aid. Charges of intervention arose frequently. Within the United States many argued that the government was

---

[36] Reston, "J.F.K.'s Sudden Diplomacy on Latin America," *New York Times*, July 27, 1962, p. 24, cited in Maher, "Kennedy and Johnson Responses," pp. 188–189.

[37] Krock, "But a Naval Patrol Is Not Invasion," *New York Times*, August 30, 1962, p. 28, cited in Maher, "Kennedy and Johnson Responses," p. 189.

Table 1

TIME SPANS BETWEEN LATIN AMERICAN COUPS D'ETAT, U.S. RECOGNITION, AND NEXT ELECTION IN COUP STATES, 1961–1963

Country	Coup d'Etat	U.S. Recognition	Time Span between Coup and Recognition (days)	Election	Time Span between Coup and Election
El Salvador	Jan. 25, 1961	Feb. 15, 1961	21	Dec. 17, 1961	10 mos., 23 days
				April 30, 1962	3 mos., 5 days
Argentina	March 29, 1962	April 18, 1962	20	July 7, 1963	1 yr., 3 mos., 9 days
Peru	July 18, 1962	Aug. 17, 1962	30	June 10, 1963	10 mos., 23 days
Guatemala	March 31, 1963	April 17, 1963	17	March 6, 1966	2 yrs., 11 mos., 6 days
Ecuador	July 11, 1963	July 31, 1963	20	Nov. 16, 1966	3 yrs., 4 mos., 5 days
Dominican Republic	Sept. 25, 1963	Dec. 14, 1963	80	June 2, 1966	2 yrs., 8 mos., 7 days
Honduras	Oct. 3, 1963	Dec. 14, 1963	72	Feb. 17, 1965	1 yr., 4 mos., 14 days
			Average 37.1		

Source: Maher, "Kennedy and Johnson Responses," p. 198.

taking moralistic, impractical approaches to the internal affairs of other states.

One conclusion stands out from a review of President Kennedy's policy. Whatever position is taken on the complex isssue of using U.S. influence to seek a return to constitutional government in Latin America, it seems clear that recognition adds nothing, indeed subtracts from the panoply of options available to U.S. policy makers. Success in attaining promises to hold elections was a result of a strong overall U.S. stance, not the result of the threat of nonrecognition. Recognition served rather as the lens through which the total U.S. response was viewed and had only that meaning that individuals and governments wished to give it. The concept of recognition presented policy makers with an either/or decision and tended to freeze the other options and shorten the time period available to construct acceptable alternatives.

Africa

Togo, 1963. The first coup that President Kennedy faced in Africa was the overthrow and murder of Sylvanus Olympio of Togo. President Kennedy reacted strongly to the coup, withholding recognition for some six months until elections were held. This action mirrored Kennedy's pursuit of the ideal of democratic government in Latin America.[38]

Olympio was assassinated early on the morning of January 13, 1963, in a coup instigated by demobilized French army veterans. In a radio broadcast the military committee indicated that the situation was under control and that it would respect all international obligations.

The U.S. refusal to grant immediate recognition to the new government in Togo resulted not only from President Kennedy's strong aversion to military dictatorships but from the strong African reaction to the overthrow of a major figure on the African political scene. Both factors pointed to withholding recognition until elections were held and until a number of African states had granted recognition. This course was in fact adopted.[39]

Congo, 1963. Some two months after President Kennedy extended formal recognition to the new government of Togo, President Youlou of the Congo (Brazzaville) was forced to resign after three days of violent demonstrations against his government. In resigning, President

---

[38] Charles Cochran, "The Recognition of States and Governments by President John F. Kennedy: An Analysis," Ph.D. diss., Tufts University, 1969, p. 224.

[39] Ibid., pp. 226–227.

Youlou entrusted power to the national Congolese army pending the establishment of a new constitution and a new government. The United States initially took the view that the events did not amount to a coup d'etat by the army but that power had passed into the most competent hands to avoid the complete breakdown of government.

However, the State Department soon advised the embassy to maintain cordial informal contact, but to "avoid any action which implies recognition."[40] The United States then delayed three months before extending recognition to the new regime, maintaining a low profile and awaiting the recognition or resumption of diplomatic relations by several major African states.

On November 12, 1963, the U.S. ambassador was authorized to notify the new regime that the U.S. government desired to extend recognition and resume normal diplomatic relations. This information was conveyed orally to the new government and no formal note was delivered. The oral conveyance of recognition represented an attempt to minimize the importance of recognition, although the United States still granted recognition explicitly, instead of simply "resuming or continuing relations."

Dahomey, 1963. The next African coup d'etat saw a renewed emphasis on elections. On October 29, 1963, Colonel Soglo, chief of Dahomey's 800-man army, seized power in a bloodless coup after striking workers had demonstrated for four days demanding President Maga's resignation. The department instructed the embassy to avoid discussion of recognition until the "promised election" was held. Elections were held in January 1964 in which a new constitution and new leaders were selected. The United States formally announced its recognition of the new government on January 31, 1964, three months after the coup.[41]

Recognition was one method the United States used to discourage military overthrows and to obtain a quick return to constitutional government through free elections in both Latin America and Africa. There is, however, a fundamental difference in the U.S. emphasis on elections in Africa and in Latin America. In Africa there is no evidence that the United States used recognition in any active way to influence the regime to hold elections. This contrasts with situations in Latin America where the United States actively bargained with the new regime over dates for elections, supervision of elections, and so on.

---

[40] U.S. Department of State, *Cablegram to Embassy*, August 17, 1963.

[41] U.S. Department of State, *Bulletin*, vol. 50 (1964), p. 238.

Republic of Korea, 1963. The first arguably extraconstitutional change of government faced by President Kennedy in the Far East occurred in South Korea in May 1961, when the democratic government headed by Chang Myon was overthrown by a military coup and replaced by a junta led by Major General Chung Hee Park and Colonel Kim Chong P'il.

The United States wished to avoid taking a formal position on the question of recognition of the new government in South Korea. The embassy continued informal contacts with representatives of the new military junta but avoided formal acts. This low-key approach left the way open for an announcement that normal relations had not been interrupted and that no formal act of recognition was necessary. Because of the strong policy considerations militating against formal recognition of the new government, the department took the position that a formal act of recognition was not necessary since the constitutional Korean head of state had not changed.[42]

Burma, 1963. In March 1963 Burmese Chief of State Ne Win deposed and imprisoned Premier U Nu and established a centralized authoritarian military regime, announcing the formation of the New Revolutionary Council and Government of the Union of Burma. The Burmese parliament was dissolved. The new regime announced that it was dedicated to the establishment of a Socialist state free from foreign influence. On March 2 the foreign office of the new regime issued a statement requesting recognition.[43]

On the same day, in a telegram to the American embassy in Rangoon, the department advised the embassy to avoid any statement implying recognition or nonrecognition of the new government, and to maintain a neutral attitude in any contacts with government officials.

On March 3 the department indicated that while there was no question of U.S. desire and intention to continue traditionally cordial relations with the new government, technical questions had arisen as to the exact legal basis of the new regime, the status of the president, and the validity of the constitution. The principal question was whether the new regime was merely a changed administration within a continuing legal framework or a new government with a break in legal continuity. The department asked the embassy's opinion on the desirability of an explicit public statement on U.S. recognition, al-

---

[42] Whiteman, *Digest of International Law*, vol. 2, p. 462.
[43] Ibid., pp. 458–459.

though no such statement had been made at the time of the 1958 army takeover in Burma.

On March 5 the embassy responded that dissolution of both chambers of parliament increased the probability that the issue of recognition would have to be faced, particularly since the term of the current president expired on March 12 and there was no provision for election of a new president except by a new parliament. Later that day the department told the embassy that it had been informed that the United Kingdom had instructed its embassy on the procedure to recognize the new regime. The United States decided to follow the same procedure, and instructed the embassy:

> Assuming you are satisfied new regime in effective control machinery of government, has general acquiescence of Burmese people, and willing and able to discharge international obligations, you may deliver to Foreign Minister note as follows—Acknowledge note from Burmese Government and desire to maintain relations between the governments. If you feel it necessary, you are authorized to state that this action in effect constitutes recognition of new government.[44]

The major foreign policy aim of the President was to maintain an independent and neutral Burma. The overthrow of U Nu was a step away from Communist influence and thus looked on with some favor by the United States. However, the basic view was that it was a purely internal political changeover that would not affect Burma's neutrality.[45] The United States did not rush to act because there was danger that quick, favorable U.S. action would compromise the Ne Win regime and make it vulnerable to charges that it was under the influence of the United States.[46]

Near East

Syria, 1961. President Kennedy was first called upon to grant recognition in the Near East in the September 1961 military insurrection in Syria. In 1958, Syria and Egypt formed the United Arab Republic. Syrians soon grew disaffected with the new republic and with the

---

[44] U.S. Department of State, *Cablegram to Rangoon*, March 5, 1962. In a press release the Department of State explained: "The note delivered by the Ambassador is an expression of recognition of the present Government of Burma by the United States Government." U.S. Department of State, *Press Release*, May 7, 1962.

[45] *New York Times*, March 5, 1962, p. 3, cited in Cochran, "Recognition of States and Governments," p. 199.

[46] Ibid., pp. 201–202.

Egyptianization of their country when the Syrian political parties were dissolved and Syrians were replaced in the government by Egyptians. On September 28, 1961, the Syrian armed forces revolted in an attempt to dissolve the republic. President Nasser sent Egyptian troops to suppress the insurrection. When the troops proved unsuccessful in quelling the revolt, Nasser, unwilling to commit more soldiers, withdrew them.[47]

The coup produced conflicting pressures for the United States. On the one hand, the United States had relatively good relations with Egypt and did not want to antagonize President Nasser by quick recognition of the Syrian regime. On the other hand Iran and Turkey, both members of the Central Treaty Organization, and pro-Western Jordan quickly recognized the new Syrian government. The United States did not wish to antagonize these friendly governments by postponing recognition.[48]

In its initial response to the revolt on September 28, the State Department took the position that the revolt was an internal affair and that the United States recognized the federation of Syria and Egypt and had friendly relations with President Nasser. On the following day the new government announced Syria's independence and said that the new regime had the support of the people. The State Department at a press briefing declared the question of recognition of the new Syrian regime to be "premature."[49]

This stance gave the United States time to reach agreement with Nasser. Nasser resolved the conflict on October 5 when he announced that he would not oppose the recognition of the government of Syria by other states. Five days later, following a communication from Kennedy to Nasser, recognition was granted:

> The United States Government, having taken note of the declaration of the Government of the Syrian Arab Republic that it intends to respect and observe its international obligations, has today, October 10, extended recognition to that

---

[47] Ibid., pp. 177–181.

[48] Ibid., pp. 184–185.

[49] *New York Times*, September 30, 1961, p. 2, cited in Cochran, "Recognition of States and Governments," p. 181. On October 1, the new regime announced that it would adhere to its international obligations and guarantee freedom of the press. In addition, the new regime pledged to restore constitutional government within four months and promised nonalignment as the basic tenet of its foreign policy. The United States received a request for recognition from the Syrian regime on October 1 (*New York Times*, October 3, 1961, p. 9, cited in Cochran, "Recognition of States and Governments," p. 184). By October 2, five nations, including three Arab states, had extended recognition in the face of Nasser's strenuous condemnation of the revolt.

Government. The Government of the Syrian Arab Republic has been apprised of the desire of the United States Government to raise to the status of an embassy the American consulate general in Damascus and to appoint Mr. Ridgway B. Knight Charge d'Affaires.[50]

In extending recognition on October 10, the United States acted only twelve days after the coup and eight days following the request for recognition.

The Soviet Union acted even more promptly, extending recognition on October 7.

Yemen, 1962. On September 27, 1962, the Yemeni army ousted Imam al-Badr a week after he succeeded to the throne on his father's death. The revolution was instigated by republican forces who actively had opposed the backward and arbitrary hereditary rule for over a decade. Imam al-Badr escaped into the mountains and rallied support for his cause. However, the republican forces gained control of most of Yemen, including the major cities and routes of communication. The United Arab Republic recognized the new government and gave it economic and military support. The Soviet Union also quickly extended recognition to the republican regime. On the other hand, Saudi Arabia and Jordan gave money and supplies to the Imam.

On October 2 the republican regime formally requested the United States to confer diplomatic recognition. The United States took the position that the question of recognition was premature given the unsettled military situation.[51]

U.S. policy makers perceived a significant national interest in Yemen, not least because several U.S. corporations had large oil holdings there. Yemen was also important from a strategic standpoint, as the United States, as well as Jordan and Saudi Arabia, feared that Yemen would fall under Egyptian dominance and would be used as a base for subversive action against states which did not favor Nasser's policies.

Delaying recognition placed the United States in a delicate position. The leaders of the republican forces warned that further delay in granting recognition could result in invalidation of agreements between Yemen and the United States. In addition, Egypt accused the United States of aiding the Imam by withholding recognition. Further,

---

[50] U.S. Department of State, *Bulletin*, vol. 45 (1961), p. 715.

[51] *New York Times*, October 2, 1962, p. 13, cited in Cochran, "Recognition of States and Governments," p. 206.

the United States was concerned that withholding recognition would force the new Yemeni government to turn to the Soviet Union for support.[52]

The military situation was unclear. The forces of the Imam were putting up strong resistance, and the republican forces were making little headway despite the presence of some 15,000 Egyptian troops. By mid-November, the Imam appeared to be gaining strength.

On October 29 the republican government again requested recognition from the United States, announcing that elections would be held soon and that communism would make no inroads in Yemen. Instead of granting recognition, President Kennedy responded by offering to use his offices to settle the conflict, proposing that Egyptian troops be withdrawn and that Jordan and Saudi Arabia cease aiding the Imam.[53] After this proved unsuccessful, the United States concluded that it would best serve U.S. interests to recognize the republican government and create an American presence in Yemen which would enable the United States to play a more effective role in settling the dispute. It was also hoped that this action would prevent the invalidation of oil agreements between Yemen and U.S. private interests.

Actual recognition followed a statement of the republican government on December 17 in which it announced its willingness to honor international obligations. It also stated that the United Arab Republic had expressed its readiness to begin the withdrawal of its forces from Yemen provided that the forces supporting the Imam withdrew and that aid to these forces was halted. The statement further guaranteed that the oil agreements would be honored. Recognition was accorded on December 19.

In a press statement on the recognition of the new regime in Yemen, the United States indicated in some detail the reasons for the decision to recognize:

> In view of a number of confusing and contradictory statements which have cast doubt upon the intentions of the new regime in Yemen, the United States Government welcomes the reaffirmation by the Yemen Arab Republic Government of its intention to honor its international obligations, of its desire for normalization and establishment of friendly relations with its neighbors, and of its intentions to concentrate on internal affairs to raise the living standards of the Yemeni people.
> The United States Government also is gratified by the

[52] Ibid., pp. 209–211.
[53] Ibid., pp. 212–213.

statesmanlike appeal of the Yemen Arab Republic to Yemenese in adjacent areas to be law-abiding citizens and notes its undertaking to honor all treaties concluded by previous Yemeni governments. This, of course, includes the Treaty of Sinai concluded with the British Government in 1934, which provides reciprocal guarantees that neither party should intervene in the affairs of the other across the existing international frontier dividing the Yemen from territory under British protection.

Further, the United States Government welcomes the Declaration of the United Arab Republic signifying its willingness to undertake a reciprocal disengagement in expeditious phased removal of troops from Yemen as external forces engaged in support of the Yemen Royalists are removed from the frontier and as external support of the Royalists is stopped.

In believing that these Declarations provide a basis for terminating the conflict over Yemen and expressing the hope that all of the parties involved in the conflict will cooperate to the end that the Yemeni people themselves be permitted to decide their own future, the United States has today [December 19] decided to recognize the Government of the Yemen Arab Republic and to extend to that Government its best wishes for success and prosperity. The United States has instructed its Charge d'Affaires in Yemen to confirm this decision in writing to the Ministry of Foreign Affairs of the Yemen Arab Republic.[54]

The U.S. action did not significantly affect the political or military situation in Yemen. This in turn led to criticism of the U.S. action. Senator Bourke Hickenlooper asked that the President consider withdrawing recognition of the republican government unless the conditions upon which recognition was granted were promptly carried out. The senator threatened to introduce a sense of the Senate resolution that recognition be withdrawn if his suggestion was not carried out by the executive branch.[55] This action prompted a response from the State Department which set out the basic policy judgment underlying the grant of recognition:

Only by recognizing the regime could we play a useful role in preventing an escalation of the Yemen conflict causing even more foreign interference and placing in serious jeopardy major U.S. economic and security interests in the Arabian Peninsula. Furthermore, our presence in Yemen . . .

---

[54] U.S. Department of State, *Bulletin*, vol. 48 (1963), pp. 11–12.
[55] Cochran, "Recognition of States and Governments," pp. 214–215.

could not have been continued for long without recognition. . . . Our essential concerns in Yemen are with: (1) keeping the Yemeni conflict and its repercussions from spreading and endangering vital U.S. and free world interests in the Near East outside of Yemen, particularly in Saudi Arabia and Jordan; (2) preventing the development by the Soviet bloc of a predominant position in Yemen; and (3) encouraging the prospects for a relatively stable and independent Yemen.[56]

Great Britain did not extend recognition because the republican forces did not have effective control of the entire country. The United States was willing to overlook this problem in order to attain political objectives.[57]

Iraq, 1963. United States and Arab interests merged at least to a limited degree in the February 1963 overthrow of the pro-Communist government of Abdul Karim Kassem in Iraq by elements of the Ba'th Party (Arab Socialist Renaissance Party). A coalition government was formed, headed by Abdul Salam Arif, a follower of President Nasser. The coup leaders were strongly anti-Communist.

Eight Arab countries—Egypt, Algeria, Jordan, Kuwait, Morocco, Syria, Yemen, and Saudi Arabia—immediately extended recognition. The United States, while favoring the overthrow of the violently anti-Western Kassem, requested assurances from the new government that it would honor its international obligations. The new government gave these assurances, promising that it would guarantee the interests

---

[56] *Congressional Record*, vol. 109, part 10, pp. 13668–13669, cited in Cochran, "Recognition of States and Governments," pp. 215–216.

[57] In October 1962, the American ambassador to Lebanon proposed that the United States adopt a clear-cut policy with respect to recognizing new governments. Under this proposal, when the question of recognition of a new government arose the U.S. government would wait thirty days, or some other specific time that might appear feasible, before taking a position on recognition. At the expiration of this period, the United States government would determine whether the traditional conditions for recognition had been fulfilled. If they had, the U.S. government would extend recognition as a matter of course without seeking to use it as a political weapon.

The department rejected this proposal, taking the position that a response to appeals for early recognition could be met just as effectively by a statement that the United States was awaiting the opportunity to assess the fulfillment of the traditional conditions. The moratorium idea had the further disadvantage of tying the hands of the United States in those cases where it might find it politically desirable, once the traditional conditions had been met, to extend recognition promptly. Also, at the expiration of the moratorium, the U.S. government would be on the spot to take a stand either to recognize or not to recognize. U.S. Department of State, Office of the Legal Adviser, Memorandum, October 1962.

of all citizens of the United States in Iraq, including oil interests. Consequently, some seventy-two hours after the overthrow the United States granted recognition:

> The United States Government, taking note of the reaffirmation by the Government of the Republic of Iraq of its intention to honor its international obligations, has today, February 11, decided to recognize the Government of Iraq and has instructed its Charge d'Affaires in Baghdad to confirm this decision in writing to the Ministry of Foreign Affaires of the Republic of Iraq.[58]

Syria, 1963. The United States took a similar position the next month, granting quick recognition in the overthrow of the existing government in Syria by leftist Ba'th Party elements in cooperation with the military. On March 8, 1963, the government of Syria, led by Prime Minister Khalid al-Azm and President Nazim al-Qudsi, was overthrown by a combination of pro-Nasser officers and Ba'thist forces. The coup met with little resistance and power was assumed by a National Council of Revolutionary Command led by Lieutenant General Lu'ay Atasi, a strong follower of Nasser. On the day of the coup, the new regime announced its willingness to honor international obligations and its intentions to follow a policy of positive neutrality.

The United States was concerned that this coup, coupled with the recent coups in Iraq and Yemen, would lead to coup attempts in pro-Western Jordan and Saudi Arabia. Nevertheless, the United States granted recognition four days after the coup:

> The United States Government, taking note of the affirmation by the Government of the Syrian Arab Republic of its intention to honor its international obligations, has today, March 12, decided to recognize the Government of the Syrian Arab Republic and has instructed its Charge d'Affaires in Damascus to confirm this decision in writing to the Ministry of Foreign Affairs of the Syrian Arab Republic. With its recognition the United States extends its best wishes for success and prosperity of the Government of the Syrian Arab Republic. . . .[59]

There was little doubt that the regime was in effective control of the country, and it had announced its intentions to honor international obligations. In addition, the United States did not want to alienate the new government by withholding recognition. Quick recognition

---

[58] Whiteman, *Digest of International Law*, vol. 2, p. 452.
[59] Ibid., pp. 455–456.

was possible here since no Middle Eastern state had taken a strong stand against recognition of the new regime.[60]

Conclusion

President Kennedy utilized recognition in what he perceived to be the national interests of the United States. In Latin America, this usually took the form of bargaining recognition for a return to constitutional government through elections. However, Kennedy did not hesitate to use recognition to obtain other objectives. In Africa as in Latin America, Kennedy saw democratic government as a stabilizing factor and a springboard to social and economic betterment. Consequently, in two of the three coups he faced in Africa, he utilized recognition in support of return to constitutional government, albeit in a more passive manner than in Latin America. In the rest of the world, especially the Near East, regional political forces shaped the use of recognition as a policy instrument. In each case, however, recognition was used to the extent possible to advance the political interests of the United States.

There can be little doubt that President Kennedy was more aggressive in his use of recognition to achieve political ends than were Presidents Johnson, Nixon, or Ford.

---

[60] Secretary Rusk commented on the grant of recognition to the new government in Syria: "We have recognized the Syrian Government because it appeared to us that it was in control of the situation and had committed itself to its own international obligations, and so forth." (Cochran, "Recognition of States and Governments," p. 193.)

3
U.S. RECOGNITION POLICY UNDER LYNDON B. JOHNSON, 1963-1968

Latin America

Recognition policy changed under Lyndon Johnson, especially in the key area of Latin America. Johnson took a more pragmatic view of the military and their seizures of power than did Kennedy. The shift in policy was not abrupt, and the United States continued to seek commitments by new regimes to constitutional government. However, recognition was withheld less often to extract this concession.

The change that came about in recognition policy under President Johnson was a consequence of a shift in attitude toward military coups d'etat. Recognition was viewed as a means to implement policy, so that once major policy changed, recognition policy changed accordingly. However, Johnson, like Kennedy, granted quick recognition or concluded that no question of recognition arose in situations where U.S. self-interest lay with the new regime.

Under Johnson "policy toward Latin America became a matter of reconciling the often conflicting goals of anti-Communism, non-involvement in domestic politics, and discouragement of the overthrow of constitutionally elected regimes."[1] In contrast to Kennedy, Johnson emphasized the goals of anti-communism and noninvolvement at the expense of constitutional rule. One scholar described the Johnson approach this way:

> Under the guidelines of pragmatism and diplomatic professionalism the United States would no longer seek to punish the armed forces in Latin America for overthrowing democratic regimes. An immediate effect would be to elimi-

---

[1] Maher, "Kennedy and Johnson Responses," p. 193.

EXTRACONSTITUTIONAL CHANGES OF GOVERNMENT IN FOREIGN STATES DURING THE PRESIDENCY OF LYNDON B. JOHNSON

Latin America

1. *Brazil, March 1964.* President Joao Goulart driven out of country, succeeded by Chamber President Mazzilli; Congress elected Humberto Castello Branco president on April 9.
2. *Bolivia, November 1964.* President Victor Paz Estenssoro forced from office by military; succeeded by Vice President Rene Barrientos Ortuno.
3. *Dominican Republic, April 1965.* Revolt overthrew ruling junta led by Donald Reid Cabral; U.S. intervened, and provisional government headed by Garcia Godoy installed in September.
4. *Ecuador, March 1966.* Military government resigned under pressure, and military high command named Clemente Yerovi as interim president.
5. *Argentina, June 1966.* President Arturo Illia removed by military, and replaced by junta which named Juan Carlos Organia president.
6. *Peru, October 1968.* Military coup ousted President Fernando Belaunde; Juan Velasco named president.
7. *Panama, October 1968.* National Guard staged coup forcing President Arnulfo Arias from office eleven days after his inauguration.

Africa

8. *Zanzibar, January 1964.* On January 12, a group of armed insurgents, in a lightning coup, overthrew the Arab sultanate.
9. *Sudan, October 1964.* After a period of rioting and unease, representatives of Sudan's armed forces and a group of civilians agreed to liquidate the existing regime and establish a new regime to be based on the 1965 provisional constitution.
10. *Algeria, June 1965.* Almed Ben Bella deposed by Colonel Houari Boumedienne.
11. *Congo, November 1965.* Joseph Kasavubu ousted by Joseph Mobutu, the chief of staff of the Congolese armed forces.
12. *Dahomey (Benin), January 1966.* General Soglo, head of the armed forces, led a coup; established Congacou as the head of a provisional government.
13. *Central African Republic (Empire), January 1966.* Colonel Bokassa deposed President David Dacko.
14. *Upper Volta, January 1966.* Colonel Lamizana deposed President Yameogo.
15. *Nigeria, 15 January 1966.* Military coup d'etat initiated by young officers; control taken by General Ironsi.

16. *Ghana, February 1966.* General Ankrah and Police Commissioner Harlley form a government following the removal of Nkrumah.
17. *Uganda, February 1966.* Prime Minister Dr. Milton Obote took over all the powers of government.
18. *Burundi, July 1966.* Prince Charles Ndizeye, heir to the throne, dismissed the government and suspended the constitution.
19. *Nigeria, July 1966.* Colonel Gowon, army chief of staff, assumed control of Nigerian government after murder of country's leader, General Ironsi.
20. *Burundi, December 1966.* Prime Minister Micombero overthrew King Ntare V and assumed full power.
21. *Togo, January 1967.* Army seized power in a bloodless coup, overthrowing President Grunitzky.
22. *Sierra Leone, March 1967.* Lieutenant Colonel Juxon-Smith headed a government which took power from Sir Albert Margai.
23. *Dahomey (Benin), December 1967.* Army officers overthrew government of President Soglo.
24. *Sierra Leone, April 1968.* A coup resulted in return to civilian rule under Siaka Stevens.
25. *Congo-Brazzaville, September 1968.* Captain Baoul assumed power, then was succeeded as president by Marien Ngouabi.
26. *Mali, November 1968.* Young officers' coup removed government of Modibo Keita.

Near East

27. *Syria, January 1966.* A moderate Ba'th government was overthrown by a group of Ba'thist military officers of the radical left.
28. *Iraq, July 1968.* The Iraqi government headed by President Abdul Salam Arif and Premier Taher Yahya was overthrown in a nearly bloodless coup mounted by a combination of "right-wing," or moderate, Ba'this.
29. *Syria, October 1968.* The prime minister and the foreign minister were removed from office as a result of policy differences within the Ba'th leadership of Syria.

Far East

30. *South Vietnam, November 1963.* General Minh overthrew regime of Ngo Dinh Diem.
31. *South Vietnam, January 1964.* General Nguyen Khanh assumed power as premier of provisional government.
32. *South Vietnam, August 1964–November 1964.* Khanh replaced Minh as chief of state. Trimvirate established under Generals Minh, Khanh, and Khiem. Triumvirate dissolved in September; Khanh resumed position of premier. Civilian government restored and Van Huong appointed premier. Revolutionary Military Council dissolved.
33. *South Vietnam, December 1964.* Khanh purged high national council.

34. *South Vietnam, January 1965.* General Khanh ousted Premier Huong.
35. *South Vietnam, June 1965.* Generals established a ruling military council, selecting General Ky as premier and General Thieu as chief of state.

Europe

36. *Greece, April 1967.* Greek military officers overthrew government of Prime Minister Kanellopoulos.
37. *Greece, December 1967.* Attempted coup by King Constantine failed; junta appointed regent who in turn appointed cabinet of military.
38. *Czechoslovakia, January 1968.* Alexander Dubcek, party secretary, and Antonin Novotny resign under intense pressure from the Soviet Union.

---

nate such deterrents against coups as denial of diplomatic relations and termination of economic aid. Moreover, the tenets of the new pragmatism would exclude the process of sharply distinguishing between constitutional governments in Latin America and military juntas. The foregoing propositions, while tempered by statements advocating political democracy, indicated a gradual change of emphasis leading to an alteration of philosophy toward military dictatorships.[2]

Dean Rusk echoed the same sentiment when, in a news conference on April 3, 1964, he said that the United States would support constitutional rule in Latin America but that it was necessary to live with states that were under military rule. The United States would not "simply walk away" from such regimes.[3]

The Johnson approach was premised on the belief that there was little the United States could do to prevent most coups d'etat and that, in any event, the United States had no mandate to interfere when Latin American governments fell short of U.S. expectations—a view reminiscent of President Franklin Roosevelt. Consequently, Johnson and his advisers rejected abstract policy in favor of a case-by-case approach in Latin America.

---

[2] Ibid. This approach is often identified with Thomas Mann who served President Johnson in the dual role of special adviser and assistant secretary of state for inter-American affairs.

[3] U.S. Department of State, "News Conference of April 3, 1964 by Secretary Rusk," *Bulletin*, vol. 50 (April 20, 1964), p. 610, quoted in Maher, "Kennedy and Johnson Responses," p. 194.

Brazil, 1964. The first Latin American military takeover Johnson faced was the overthrow of President Joao Goulart in Brazil in late March 1964, a change the United States welcomed. On April 2, two days before Goulart left Brazil, President Johnson gave his "warmest wishes" to President Mazzilli. On April 24, Secretary of State Dean Rusk expressed his satisfaction with the coup. The assistant secretary of state for inter-American affairs, Thomas Mann, put it even more strongly, invoking the domino theory toward coups in Latin America:

> We are not at all sorry when we see a neighbor put out a fire in his house. Fires have a way of spreading. And I am sure that all of our friends know they can continue to count on us for help if they should be threatened by communist subversion.[4]

Another commentator explained the "Mann Doctrine" this way:

> At a meeting of the United States ambassadors to Latin America, the new Assistant Secretary of State for Latin American Affairs, Thomas Mann, reportedly suggested that it was unwise for the United States to continue to become involved in internal threats to freedom in Latin America, since Kennedy's policies had demonstrated how fruitless it was for the United States to try to impose democracy upon Latin America. Mann urged that greater attention be paid to immediate national security interests, such as protection of United States investments and resistance to communism. He suggested less passionate commitment to political freedom and social justice. The emerging "Mann Doctrine" seemed to be that henceforth the United States would no longer oppose military coups or rightist dictatorships. Thus, the new, and much narrower criteria for recognizing and supporting new governments in Latin America seemed to be anti-communism and security for foreign investments. Eliminated were the Kennedy foreign policy dimensions of human freedom and social justice. The United States seemed to be returning to the hard-nosed pragmatism that had characterized its foreign policy in Latin America between the end of World War II and 1960.[5]

Formally, the United States took the view that a recognition question did not arise on the military takeover in Brazil because the constitutional thread was unbroken. Mazzilli had been installed as

---

[4] Thomas C. Mann, "The Alliance for Progress," U.S. Department of State, *Bulletin*, vol. 50 (June 1, 1964), p. 858, quoted in Maher, "Kennedy and Johnson Responses," p. 193.

[5] Lieuwen, *Generals vs. Presidents*, p. 143.

president of Brazil after the congress had expressed its approval. The revolt also had been supported by the president of the senate in the chamber of deputies, by the governors of key states, and by the military.[6] Secretary Rusk reflected this view in a news conference:

> Mazzilli has been installed as president of Brazil after congress so voted. The senate declared the office vacant. This culminates the revolt by democratic forces in Brazil, supported by the president of the senate in a chamber of deputies, by the governors of key states, and by the military. This is not at all a military coup in the sense that the continuity of civilian government, the constitution, and democratic processes are being preserved. Resistance took shape after Goulart attacked the constitution and congress.[7]

Various Latin American governments took the same view. Chile replied to the Brazilian note on April 7, effecting recognition. Peru took the position that, as with Goulart, the new president had been constitutionally installed and there was no need for recognition of the new government. Peru instructed its minister to carry on business as usual with the new government. Bolivia recognized the Brazilian regime on April 18. Uruguay approved the acceptance note from Brazil on April 24, signifying a continuance of relations. In contrast, Venezuela and Costa Rica took their usual position against recognition of military regimes that overthrew democratically elected governments. Costa Rica did modify its position because the newly selected president had some constitutional claim to the position.

Strong political interests lay behind the U.S. judgment not to raise the question of recognition. The United States had long been concerned with President Goulart's softness on communism and with his unsound economic policies. Consequently, the United States favored the change of government and "side-stepped" the recognition issue.[8]

Bolivia, 1964. On November 4, the commander-in-chief of the armed forces ousted Paz Estenssoro. Control of the government was assumed by General Ovando. General Barrientos, the vice-president, subsequently supplanted Ovando and assumed sole presidential powers.

---

[6] The *New York Times* on April 7, 1964, criticized the U.S. action: "To make such a public show of rejoicing, even before the situation had clarified, has given the world the impression—an entirely wrong one—that the United States had something to do with the coup."

[7] U.S. Department of State, "News Conference of April 3, 1964 by Secretary Rusk," *Bulletin* (April 20, 1964), p. 610.

[8] Lieuwen, *Generals vs. Presidents*, p. 143.

On November 7, the new Bolivian government informed the United States that the junta had taken control of the government of Bolivia, that it was in full control of the country, and that it intended to abide by Bolivia's international commitments and desired to maintain relations with the United States and other friendly countries. Following the coup the United States had maintained informal contacts with representatives of the junta to protect American lives and property, but had emphasized to the new regime that this in no way implied an intention to recognize. The United States sought information from the junta to assist it in determining whether the junta was in control of the country with the general assent of the population.

The United States postponed recognition for a month, although in doing so it risked losing its influence on the new regime. However, because further delay might have injured future relations with the new government of Bolivia and because most American states had already acted, the United States granted recognition on December 7,[9] and released the following press statement:

> The Department of State has instructed our Ambassador in La Paz, Douglas Henderson, to acknowledge the note of the Foreign Minister of Bolivia dated November the 7th, 1964. By means of this acknowledgement the United States is renewing normal relations with Bolivia under the military junta of government, which is presided over by General Barrientos.
>
> The United States Government has ascertained that the military junta is in effective control of the government and the country, and that it has pledged itself to fulfill Bolivia's international obligations. The United States Government has noted the declaration of the president of the junta made public on November 6th, and reiterated subsequently, that preparation for democratic elections would begin shortly, and that elections would be held soon toward the early restoration of constitutional government.
>
> The United States decision was taken after consultation with other governments of this hemisphere and elsewhere and following similar action by a number of them.[10]

---

[9] One commentator found several reasons for grant of recognition: "The State Department let it be known that the Barrientos regime had also rendered itself worthy of recognition by retaining technically competent people of all parties in government positions, by respecting the rights of trade unions, by trying to collect arms in the possession of civilians, and by taking a clear stand against communism and communist China." Dozier, "Recognition in Contemporary Inter-American Relations," *Journal of Inter-American Studies*, vol. 8 (1966), p. 143.

[10] Department of State, *Press Release*, December 7, 1964.

The press statement represented a subtle shift in U.S. policy. Instead of formally granting recognition, the United States announced that it had "renewed normal relations." Although mention continued to be made of the commitment to return to constitutional government, less attention was devoted to the attainment of this end, and more attention was devoted to deemphasizing the recognition process. This policy was later developed to the point that the United States would merely continue relations when a coup occurred, rather than suspend relations only to "renew" them a short time later.

Dominican Republic, 1965. The United States involvement in the revolutionary situation in April 1965, in the Dominican Republic is well known and hotly debated. While it constitutes the apogee of U.S. involvement in the 1960s in the affairs of a Latin American country, it offers little insight into the development of recognition policy. It does, however, afford an illustration of a situation in which the United States went well beyond the use of recognition to influence the affairs of a Latin American state.

After months of negotiations, on September 2 a provisional government headed by Hector Garcia Godoy, who had been foreign minister in Juan Bosch's cabinet, was set up. On September 3, the new provisional government of the Dominican Republic informed American nations of the installation of a provisional government under President Godoy, and requested recognition of the new regime. The new government guaranteed law and order, the free exercise of rights to all citizens, and compliance with the international commitments assumed by the nation. The United States accorded recognition on the same day.[11]

OAS Resolution XXVI. At the Second Special Inter-American Conference in Rio de Janeiro on November 17-30, 1965, the Assembly adopted Resolution XXVI, which provided an informal procedure for the recognition of de facto governments. Resolution XXVI recommended to member states that they begin an exchange of views on the situation immediately after the overthrow of a government and its replacement by a de facto government. The resolution further stated that once opinions have been exchanged, each government must decide whether it will maintain diplomatic relations with the de facto government. It did not specifically deal with the question whether relations are suspended and need to be reestablished with the new regime, or whether relations continue unless broken.

---

[11] Department of State, *U.S. Policy toward Latin America*, pp. 94–95.

Adoption of Resolution XXVI inserted a new factor into the process of granting recognition to American states following a coup. However, the resolution did not significantly change recognition practice.

Ecuador, 1966. The United States deemphasized recognition in response to the coup in Ecuador in 1966, when the three-man ruling junta turned over its power to the army high command. The military high command consulted with prominent political figures and named Clemente Yerovi as provisional president. Yerovi was a wealthy, liberal Guayaquil businessman who had been associated with President Plaza. Yerovi named a civilian cabinet of twelve businessmen to replace the military cabinet and the provisional military government. He cancelled the upcoming elections, stated that he would call a convention to draw up a new constitution, and instigated a major military shake-up, while retaining the army's support.

As a result of quick recognition by Chile and Peru, the United States decided to continue relations with the new government of Ecuador, and on April 12 a note was delivered to the Ecuadorean foreign ministry expressing the desire of the United States to continue relations. Recognition was not explicitly mentioned in the note. However, in the press release accompanying the note the Department of State acknowledged that the note constituted recognition.[12]

Argentina, 1966. A comparable formula was used in the response to the overthrow of President Arturo Illia of Argentina in June 1966. One commentator, Theodore Maher, in comparing the U.S. response to the Argentine coup with the response to the Brazilian coup in 1964, noted that the Argentine coup "produced a somewhat stronger though by no means harsh response from the Johnson administration."[13] Maher also reports that the United States made efforts to prevent the coup, including advance pressure on rebel leaders and promises of equipment for government forces. The junta generals, however, were not dissuaded.[14]

Although the United States finally expressed its desire "to maintain" normal relations with the new regime, before it took this action it made strenuous efforts to persuade the new military regime to promise that it would hold elections and requested other nations to delay recognition until the assurance was obtained.

---

[12] U.S. Department of State, *Press Release*, April 12, 1966.
[13] Maher, "Kennedy and Johnson Responses," p. 195.
[14] Ibid.

In constructing a policy position on the Argentine coup, the United States faced the dilemma of reconciling recognition of a military regime with overall hemispheric policy, especially the objectives of the Alliance for Progress. On the one hand, the United States did not wish to antagonize a government that it might have to deal with for some time. On the other hand, it did not wish to give critics any arguments against U.S. economic and military programs, which were deemed essential to the achievement of mutual goals in the hemisphere. Initially, the U.S. posture on recognition of Argentina was well received, both in the United States and in Latin America.

In the press briefing on June 28, the State Department stated that it was greatly concerned over the displacement of democratic government and the rupture of constitutional processes in an OAS member state. It also stated that, in keeping with international practice in such cases, it would suspend diplomatic relations, and consult with other OAS members in accordance with Resolution XXVI of the 1965 Rio Conference.[15] Although the United States did suspend relations, it continued the Food for Peace program, and health and educational aid, diluting the harshness of the response.[16]

The coup hurt prospects for U.S. programs in Latin America. Critics were arguing that the Alliance for Progress was failing and that U.S. military assistance programs were a mistake because they led to coups such as the one in Argentina. Consequently, whatever the new regime in Argentina did to indicate publicly its intentions to return to constitutional democracy would smooth the way for the United States to resume relations.

In order to gain time to obtain a commitment to constitutional government and to forestall quick recognition by a major Latin American state, the United States invoked the Resolution XXVI procedures. Resolution XXVI of the Rio Conference envisioned prior consultations among OAS states before any individual action was taken and recommended that an exchange of views consider, among other things, whether a new government proposed to hold elections, respect human rights, and comply with the Charter of Punte del Este. It was plain that the new government was in complete control and that

---

[15] In formulating its position, the fundamental differences between the Brazilian revolution of 1964 and the Argentine coup were significant to the United States. In the former case, in the U.S. view, Goulart had actively subverted the constitution in collaboration with Communist elements. The Brazilian revolution was designed to stop this in the interest of preserving basic democratic institutions. In the U.S. view, these factors were not present in the Argentine situation.

[16] Maher, "Kennedy and Johnson Responses," p. 195.

the overthrow did not take place with the complicity of any foreign government. The new government had also stated its intention to fulfill international obligations. However, it had made no definite public comment on elections, civil liberties, and human rights.

Brazil took the position that Resolution XXVI of the Rio Conference was not applicable since it was intended to apply only to de facto governments influenced by extracontinental powers and therefore potentially dangerous to the security of the Western Hemisphere. In any case, Brazil felt that the government of Argentina had met two of the three conditions of Resolution XXVI, namely, freedom from foreign links and fulfillment of international obligations, and there was no reason to doubt the government's disposition to normalize Argentine institutional life within a reasonable period. Further, a delay in recognition would create justified resentment in the new government of Argentina.

Venezuela urged convocation of an informal meeting of foreign ministers, hinting at some form of collective sanction. Columbia, Peru, Chile, and Uruguay all wanted more clear-cut indications from the government of Argentina on its intentions. These states were anxious, however, not to delay excessively in order to avoid antagonizing the regime with which they would have to live.

The leader of the new government made speeches on July 12 and 13 on the plans and objectives of the government. The United States considered these speeches as an indication that the new government intended to respect human rights, maintain friendly relations with its neighbors, and move toward the restoration of democratic representative government. The statements were not as categorical as the United States desired nor did they provide a timetable for return to representative government. Nevertheless, they did indicate a degree of affirmative response on the part of the Argentine government to the criteria of Resolution XXVI. As a result the United States delivered a note to the new Argentine government on July 15 in which it indicated its desire to maintain traditional relations. Recognition was not specifically mentioned.

The U.S. interest in the commitment to a return to constitutional government via free elections was still apparent in the response to the Argentine coup. However, there was a growing unwillingness to press hard for such a commitment. The United States was careful to avoid being boxed into a rigid position (in demanding free elections) that would preclude recognition if it could not gain its objectives. The public announcement that the United States finally accepted did not provide a timetable for elections to return a constitutional government, but, in the U.S. view, the statements amounted to an acceptable degree of affirmative response to the criteria of Resolution XXVI.[17]

The "comparatively mild" U.S. response to the Argentine coup and the earlier Bolivian coup drew criticism, with some contending that the U.S. recognition policy resulted in the "too easy acceptance of authoritarian governments in the name of anti-communism."[18]

Peru, 1968. The United States continued its hybrid policy in responding to the October 1968 military coup in Peru, officially suspending relations, then resuming them in an official statement some twenty-three days after the coup. By that time, some thirty-six of the forty countries having diplomatic relations with Peru had acted, including all OAS states except Venezuela, the Dominican Republic, and El Salvador.

Initially, the United States reacted negatively to the coup, noting that the military regime had said nothing about plans to return to an elected government. The State Department announced that much was still unclear about the nature of the regime and the precise policies it would follow, and that these matters were of great concern to the U.S. government and would be carefully considered in any decision on the resumption of relations. Concern had also been expressed by Latin American nations. The United States was "particularly discourag[ed]" by the Peruvian coup in light of the relative stability in Latin America throughout 1967 and most of 1968.[19]

The new government of Peru asked for the continuance of relations in a diplomatic note. The United States responded to the junta note by requesting answers to various questions, specifically whether the revolutionary government intended to make any statements regarding the points covered by Resolution XXVI. The State Department also was concerned about the abrogation by the military junta of an agreement made between the previous government and the International Petroleum Company, a subsidiary of the Standard Oil Company.[20]

---

[17] With the adoption of Resolution XXVI, the United States, in communicating with a new regime, no longer had to advance, unilaterally, criteria that the regime had to meet before the United States could grant recognition. With Resolution XXVI available, the United States could merely refer to the criteria set up in it, and thus rebut the charge that it was setting up its own political criteria for recognition and intervening in the political process of a sovereign state. Resolution XXVI, of course, contains the usual criteria advanced by the United States, including a return to constitutional government via free elections.

[18] Maher, "Kennedy and Johnson Responses," p. 195.

[19] Ibid., p. 196.

[20] Ibid.

The United States evidently received satisfactory responses to these questions, for a note was delivered on October 25 resuming relations. U.S. officials cited both the assurance given by the Peruvian government to fulfill traditional obligations and its public statement regarding a return to constitutional rule through a constitutional referendum.

> The American Embassy in Lima advised the Peruvian Ministry of Foreign Affairs at noon today [October 25] that the United States Government has resumed diplomatic relations with the Government of Peru.
>
> The United States decision was based on an analysis and study of the consultations we carried on with other OAS [Organization of American States] countries under OAS Resolution 26 [adopted by the Second Special Inter-American Conference at Rio de Janeiro on November 30, 1965]; and another consideration: Peru had publicly made the traditional guarantees of its recognition of international obligations and has indicated its intention to return to constitutional government.[21]

At the time the United States acted, all non-American republics with whom Peru traditionally maintained relations had recognized or continued relations.

The United States officially suspended relations with Peru after the coup. The State Department in announcing the resumption of relations reported that foreign aid, suspended at the time of the coup, remained under review. Because of the expropriation question, the United States went beyond seeking a *pro forma* statement to honor international obligations, and sought assurances that Peru would honor international obligations to the nationals of other states and their property.

Panama, 1968. In an October 1968 coup, the National Guard, Panama's army, overthrew President Arnulfo Arias. The United States officially suspended relations on October 12. On November 13 it announced that it was resuming diplomatic relations. In the interim, the United States sought assurances, as it had in the Peruvian case, of Panama's willingness to comply with the substantive premises of Resolution XXVI.

On October 15 the department spokesman, Robert McCloskey, reviewed the status of U.S. relations with Panama. He indicated that relations had been suspended as a result of the events in Panama, but

---

[21] U.S. Department of State, *For the Press*, October 24, 1968.

not by any affirmative act by the United States. He further stated that at this point Resolution XXVI was applicable and referred to the secretary's previous statement of concern over the breakdown of constitutional government in Panama.[22]

In a press statement on October 16, McCloskey stated that during the period of suspended relations it was routine that U.S. assistance programs be taken under review. After a period of assessment, the United States would make its decision on the status of its relations with Panama. Answering questions from the press, McCloskey avoided use of the term recognition, focusing instead on diplomatic relations.[23]

In response to the U.S. concerns, the junta appointed members of a new electoral tribunal, promised to hold elections, relaxed the ban on publication of certain newspapers suppressed at the time of the coup, and reinstated on November 8 the suspended constitutional guarantees for due process in the courts, ex post facto laws and the prohibition of the death penalty and the confiscation of property. However, other constitutional guarantees, including habeas corpus, remained suspended.

On November 13, as a result of the steps taken by the junta, the United States transmitted a note to the foreign minister of Panama announcing the continuation of relations. The word "recognition" was not used in the note.

> The American Embassy in Panama City advised the Panamanian Foreign Ministry at nine a.m. today that the United States was resuming diplomatic relations with Panama. The United States took this action after extensive consultations with other members of the Organization of American States, in accordance with Resolution XXVI of the Second Special Inter-American Conference. In the course of these consultations we have given careful consideration to the publicly declared intention of the Panama Government to hold elections, to return to constitutional government, to respect human rights, and to observe Panama's international obligations. The Panamanian Government has taken

---

[22] U.S. Department of State, *Statement by Robert McCloskey*, October 15, 1968. On October 12, Secretary Rusk issued a statement: "We are deeply distressed to learn that the Panamanian National Guard has overthrown the recently inaugurated President, Dr. Arnulfo Arias. This action to remove a constitutionally elected Chief of State is of profound concern to the United States. We have a close relationship with Panama and a stake in the stability of the isthmus in view of our presence there as stewards of the vital Panama Canal. This coup d'etat must be equally disturbing to our sister republics in the hemisphere." U.S. Department of State, *For the Press*, October 12, 1968.

[23] U.S. Department of State, *For the Press*, October 16, 1968.

the first steps toward carrying out these intentions by constituting a tribunal to prepare procedures and regulations for future elections and by restoring some of the constitutional guarantees suspended at the time of the coup. We have also noted that the decree restoring these guarantees reiterates the firm intention of the Government to restore full constitutional rights promptly and to hold free elections.[24]

At the time the United States announced continuance of relations with Panama, thirty-three days after the coup, the majority of OAS states had already acted. Ecuador, Venezuela, and three Central American republics were the principal exceptions.

Africa

After an initial transition period, African recognition policy under President Johnson became virtually automatic, at least toward the "usual" African coup d'etat. The policy reflected the perception that U.S. interests were best served by maintaining contact and diplomatic relations with whatever regime was in control of the governmental machinery of an African state. It also underlined the lack of influence the United States had in post-coup situations in Africa in the mid-1960s.

Zanzibar, 1964. The coup in January 1964 in Zanzibar presented policy makers with a particularly difficult situation. The new junta ordered the U.S. diplomatic personnel to leave Zanzibar unless the U.S. government extended recognition to the new regime. When this recognition was not forthcoming, U.S. officials were expelled on January 12. Eleven days later, the United States delivered a note of recognition.[25] Pressures against the new regime and the desire of the United States to weaken Communist influence brought about the prompt, explicit recognition of the new government.

Australia, Canada, New Zealand, and Pakistan extended recognition promptly. Consultations with these countries had been one of the factors that held up British recognition of the new government, and the United States deferred to Great Britain on the matter of recognition. The Soviet Union, Communist China, and other Soviet bloc nations extended quick recognition to the regime.

Here the United States unmistakably used recognition for politi-

---

[24] U.S. Department of State, *For the Press*, November 13, 1968.

[25] A press statement announcing informal recognition was released in Washington on January 25. U.S. Department of State, *For the Press*, January 25, 1964.

cal purposes. However, the political goal sought by the grant of recognition differed from that sought by Kennedy in Togo. In the 1963 coup in Togo the purpose of withholding recognition was to foster the holding of free elections; in the 1964 coup in Zanzibar the aim of the prompt recognition was to weaken Communist influence.

In Africa, the United States did not engage in explicit bargaining to gain the quid pro quo for the grant of recognition as occurred in Latin America during this period. Recognition was used solely as a passive tool.

Sudan, 1964. Another aspect of the U.S. response to an arguably extraconstitutional change of government was illustrated by the coup in Sudan in October 1964. Here the new regime took the position that it was merely reinstating the constitution of 1958 and that therefore the question of recognition did not arise. The United States agreed with this interpretation and normal contacts were continued with the new regime.

This action by the United States reflects a pattern that developed later in the 1960s in response to coups in both Latin America and Africa, and indeed, the world. If there were enough elements of continuity between the old and new regimes, and the United States either had a minimal interest in the change of government or favored the new regime, policy makers would proclaim that the question of recognition did not arise. In most cases, this did not involve a sophisticated analysis of the foreign state's constitution or domestic law. It was, rather, a policy judgment to downplay recognition where any elements of continuity were present and as such constituted a harbinger of American recognition policy in the 1970s.

Algeria, 1965. A continuing deemphasis of recognition marked the U.S. response to the coup d'etat in Algeria on June 19, 1965, in which President Ben Bella was overthrown by the army. On July 5, the British government announced the acceptance of the revolutionary regime as the legal government of Algeria. Its announcement stated that the change of government resulting from the overthrow of President Ben Bella required no formal act of recognition, and consequently diplomatic relations had not been interrupted by the Algerian coup. Nevertheless, some African countries in the British Commonwealth decided to withhold recognition from the new regime which they viewed as unconstitutional.

The United States communicated its intention to resume relations to Algeria leaders on June 30. On July 5, the anniversary of Algerian independence, messages of congratulations were delivered on behalf of President Johnson and Secretary Rusk to the leaders of the new regime. There was no formal announcement of recognition.

The U.S. response to the coup is significant because it represented the first major occasion in Africa in which the United States moved away from an explicit grant of recognition to a mere resumption of relations, thereby reducing the importance of recognition and downplaying its significance. Later in the decade the United States adopted this approach and applied it consistently to African coups.

Congo, 1965. The deemphasis of recognition continued in the United States response to the November 1965 coup in the Congo where Joseph Kasavubu was ousted by Joseph Mobutu, the chief of staff of the Congolese armed forces. Belgium, the former colonial ruler, promptly accepted General Mobutu as president of the Congo. France quickly recognized General Mobutu's regime. The Indian government recognized the new government on December 1. Nigeria, the first African country to act, recognized the new government on December 4.

The United States followed its normal policy of waiting for African leadership to act before establishing normal relations with the new regime. On December 7, the U.S. ambassador was advised to tell Mobutu that the United States would deal with his government and that no formal act of recognition would be made. The ambassador conveyed this message on the same day.

Dahomey, 1966. A rash of coups occurred in Africa in the period January–February 1966. In one case, there was enough continuity for the United States to say that no question of recognition arose. In other instances, the United States followed its newly adopted policy of resuming relations and avoiding public recognition where possible. In still other cases, the United States announced that relations were continuing with no interruption. In only one case did the United States, for political reasons, explicitly recognize the new government. The first of the rash of coups occurred in early January in Dahomey, following two months of unrest. The coup was led by Colonel Soglo, chief of staff of the army, who had become impatient over the country's political instability.

Some three weeks later, on January 28, 1966, the State Department's spokesman said in a press conference that there had been no interruption in the conduct of our relations with Dahomey, and that recognition had continued.

Central African Republic, 1966. The technique of avoiding public recognition was used in the January 1, 1966, overthrow of President

Dacko in the Central African Republic. On January 28, a spokesman for the Department of State said, "We are still studying the situation."[26] On February 9, the spokesman said, "We continue to have normal communications and diplomatic exchanges with these governments [Upper Volta and Central African Republic], but we are still studying the question of whether the technical question of diplomatic recognition comes up."[27] On March 4, in connection with a press statement, department spokesmen confirmed normalization of diplomatic relations between the United States and the Central African Republic.[28]

The United States adopted a similar approach in responding to the January overthrow of President Congacou of Dahomey (Benin), concluding that there was "no interruption in the conduct of our relations with Dahomey. Recognition has continued."[29]

In responding to the January 4 coup in Upper Volta, the department announced: "In view of the fact that normal communications between our two governments have been maintained, the U.S. government believes that the question of recognition does not arise."[30]

The shift towards the "automatic" policy of recognition in African coups was quite apparent by early 1966. State Department policy makers never announced that they had adopted an automatic policy. Nevertheless, in the "usual" African military takeover, recognition was virtually automatic if it formally was granted at all. As time progressed, the State Department became more sophisticated in evading questions about recognition from the press, where the issue usually arose. Such phrases as "relations are continuing," "there has been no interruption in our relations with [the foreign state]," and "the question of recognition does not arise" became as familiar a litany as the news that another military takeover had occurred in Africa. The similarity of the U.S. approach toward African coups to the approach embodied in the Estrada Doctrine discussed in the introduction is striking.

Nigeria, 1966. A group of army officers attempted a coup in Nigeria on January 15, 1966. They succeeded in killing a number of important government officials, including the prime minister. However, the majority of the army remained loyal to the federal government, and General Ironsi, the chief of staff, was able to subdue the uprising.

---

[26] Ibid., January 28, 1966.

[27] U.S. Department of State, *Press Conference*, February 9, 1966.

[28] Ibid., March 4, 1966.

[29] Ibid., January 28, 1966.

[30] Ibid., February 10, 1966.

On January 16, General Ironsi announced the suspension of major provisions in the Nigerian constitution and the formation of an interim military government to maintain law and order in the country. The military governors were to be appointed in each of Nigeria's four regions and would be responsible to the federal military government for maintaining law and order.

On January 17 the Nigerian rebels announced that they had set up a revolutionary government in Kaduna. In Accra, President Nkrumah of Ghana announced that his government had decided to accord full diplomatic recognition to the federal military provisional government of Nigeria.

On January 19, the Nigerian ambassador in Washington presented the department with a note informing the department that the council of ministers had unanimously decided to hand over control of government to Major General Ironsi. The note described Ironsi's decree of January 16 and added that the ministry hoped, in view of the pledge given by the military government to continue diplomatic relations and to honor all treaty obligations, that relations between Nigeria and the U.S. government could continue to be normal and cordial. The government of Nigeria's note requested formal acknowledgement by the department.

On January 26, in an outgoing telegram, the department informed the embassy that it had concluded that the question of recognition did not arise.[31] Accordingly, the United States planned to acknowledge receipt of the government of Nigeria's note without mentioning recognition. The department stated that it was making an effort to play recognition problems in as low a key as possible. On January 28 the department's spokesmen said in reply to a number of questions that "the United States has maintained and expects to continue to maintain diplomatic relations with the government of Nigeria. We have been studying all facts available and we consider that the question of recognition does not arise."[32]

Ghana, 1966. President Nkrumah of Ghana was overthrown by an army and police coup on February 24, 1966, when he was out of the country on a state visit to various Communist capitals. The coup set off a mixed reaction throughout Africa. Mali and Congo-Brazzaville condemned the overthrow of President Nkrumah as part of a general offensive by imperialist forces against the young states of Africa.

The State Department, in a telegram on February 26, informed

[31] U.S. Department of State, *Telegram, Washington to Lagos,* January 26, 1966.
[32] U.S. Department of State, *Press Conference,* January 28, 1966.

the embassy that the problem of recognition of the new regime in Ghana differed in important respects from that involved in Nigeria and other recent African turnovers, mainly in the absence of even a pretext of constitutional continuity between the previous government and the National Liberation Council. The telegram further stated that the United States intended an early decision on recognition but preferred that African countries take the lead.

Politically, the department was encouraged by the composition of the new government. Nevertheless, on February 25, at a press briefing, the department's spokesman stated that it was too early to comment on recognition. In a memorandum of March 3 to the secretary, the Bureau of African Affairs urged recognition, as did the U.S. ambassador to Ghana. The memo noted that the National Liberation Council was in complete control and had the enthusiastic support of the vast majority of Ghanaians and that it was in the national interest to recognize. The memo argued that the United States should not be the first country to recognize and that other countries, particularly African countries, should take the lead. A number of states had already recognized or were in the process of recognizing. As of March 3, Liberia, Nigeria, Upper Volta, Togo, Dahomey, and the Ivory Coast had formally recognized. The Malagasy Republic, Senegal, and Tunisia indicated that they would follow the practice of recognizing states rather than governments and that this applied to Ghana.

On March 4, in an outgoing telegram, the State Department noted that it had received a routine note from the Ghanaian embassy advising of a delay in its ambassador's return to Washington. The United States acknowledged the note on the same day, addressing the Ghanaian chargé in his official capacity and stating that the United States hoped for continuation of friendly and mutually beneficial relations between the governments and peoples of Ghana and the United States. The department authorized the embassy in Accra to inform the National Liberation Council of this action and that it constituted recognition.[33]

Great Britain announced recognition of the Ghanaian regime on March 4. The Australian government recognized the Ghanaian government on March 5 and Japan recognized on March 9. On the other hand, Mali indicated that it intended to give Nkrumah total and resolute support.

The action by the United States was somewhat of a surprise in that recognition was emphasized and the word *recognition* was used without prompting from the press. This was a political judgment that

---

[33] U.S. Department of State, *Telegram, Washington to Accra,* March 4, 1966.

such action would be productive under the circumstances. However, in emphasizing recognition the United States did not attempt to use it as an active policy tool, as it did in Latin America. Instead, as in the Sudan earlier, a judgment was made that the explicit grant of recognition might have a beneficial effect. Such use, however, was the exception and did not change what was coming to be a uniform recognition policy toward Africa.

During this period of numerous coups, the African bureau of the State Department and its lawyers generated a number of internal memoranda to develop U.S. policy. These papers accurately reflected the thinking of the policy officials on recognition questions in the African area. In February 1966, in response to a general paper on recognition policy, a legal adviser to the African bureau stated:

> As you know, L/AF [Office of the Assistant Legal Adviser for African Affairs] has for the past year favored the use of the term "normalization of relations" as opposed to recognition. I think this is more than a semantic distinction. We are frequently placed in an awkward position by our traditional recognition policies. New regimes which have come to power by coup, as well as the press and general public, expect us to make some formal statement about recognition. We are often reluctant to do so because of either the instability of the new regime, the way it has come to power, our relations with the government it deposed, or the uncertain course of future events. On the other hand, we frequently fear not doing what is expected of us, since it might lead the new regime to believe we are lukewarm towards it.
>
> To avoid these problems, we have tried to talk in terms of the continuance of diplomatic relations rather than recognition. In the six African coups which have occurred in the past year (Algeria, Congo, Dahomey, Upper Volta, Central African Republic and Nigeria), we have requested our Embassy to study the situation closely and have phrased our reaction to meet the situation. In certain cases we have instructed our Ambassador to avoid formal acts of a signing of new agreements. In others we have instructed our posts to continue normal contacts while avoiding formal acts. In still others we have told the new regimes that we regard our diplomatic relations as continuous or as having continued without interruption. In none of these instances have we made any formal statement of recognition. In each case, as the new regime has consolidated its powers, we have authorized our Embassy to undertake new commitments, to assure the new leaders of our support, or to respond to the press or other inquiries by saying that our relations with the

new government are normal. In the Nigerian case, after a couple of weeks we responded to a press question—Does this mean we recognize the new regime—by saying simply yes. I believe that the course of action that we have followed in Africa has been effective and consistent.[34]

In mid-February 1966 a cable was drawn up for all African diplomatic posts concerning the application in Africa of U.S. policies toward diplomatic representation and recognition. The purpose of the cable was to facilitate consistent application of established policy in the event of coups d'etat. It called for the continued deemphasis of recognition and set up a procedure for handling the American response to coups.

Uganda, 1966. The policy set forth in the cable was applied to the February 2, 1966, coup in Uganda in which the prime minister, Dr. Milton Obote, took over all the powers of government. Given the elements of continuity between the old and new Ugandan regimes, the State Department concluded that no question of recognition arose. On March 11, in an outgoing telegram, the department stated its belief that the internal Ugandan constitutional problem did not raise a question of recognition. The ambassador was accredited to the government headed by Obote that still existed, and consequently the department did not consider that relations were suspended. The act of signing a Public Law 480 wheat agreement with the government of Uganda as one of the signatories was consonant with this interpretation.

Burundi, 1966. No significant U.S. interests were involved in the overthrow of King Mwambutsa IV of Burundi by his son in July 1966. On July 8, Prince Charles Ndizeye of Burundi, the twenty-year-old heir to the throne, announced that he had dismissed the government and suspended the constitution, and that he would govern by royal decree in order to check the growing anarchy, chaos, and nepotism in the kingdom. He did not, however, formally depose his father, King Mwambutsa IV, who was abroad and had been in Europe for almost a year. The new government received recognition from the Congo-Kinshasa, and the Belgian government delivered its good wishes to the new regime.

On July 14, in a telegram to the American embassy in Burundi,

---

[34] U.S. Department of State, Office of the Legal Adviser, Memorandum from Assistant Legal Adviser for African Affairs to legal adviser re recognition policy toward African coups d'etat. February 1966.

the department noted that since the new government had not raised the recognition issue, the embassy should avoid addressing itself directly to the question as long as possible. If asked, the embassy was instructed to state that the U.S. government intended to continue normal diplomatic contacts with the government of Burundi and would study the situation. The embassy was requested to carry on business as usual with the new government but told to seek instructions from the department if formal acts became necessary.

On July 21, in another outgoing telegram, the department agreed with the embassy view that the United States should not become conspicuous by standing aloof in view of the affirmative actions taken by Belgium and the Congo and other foreign governments with missions in Burundi. Although the direction the new government would take was not clear, the department felt the benefit of doubt should be given to the new Burundi leaders. As a result, the department instructed the ambassador to advise the foreign minister of Burundi that the United States intended to continue normal relations.

In December, the prime minister, Captain Michel Micombero, and other army officers assumed full powers after overthrowing the prince, who had become King Ntare V. Captain Micombero declared himself president and dissolved the old government in favor of a Provisional Revolutionary Committee of thirteen officers which would rule until a new government could be formed. King Ntare was in the Congo at the time of the overthrow. Given the low level of U.S. interests and the elements of continuity, the State Department concluded that no question of recognition arose.

Nigeria, 1966. A more significant coup d'etat occurred in Nigeria in July 1966. On July 29, a mutiny in the army began and dissident troops seized and killed the country's leader, Major General Ironsi. The dissident army unit leader, Lieutenant Colonel Gowon, army chief of staff, announced on August 1, following three days of national anxiety over the mutiny, that he had assumed control of the Nigerian government and armed forces with the support of a majority of members of the Supreme Military Council.

On August 5 in Washington the Nigerian ambassador to the United States announced a press conference. The State Department noted in a memorandum that the ambassador would inform the press that Lieutenant Colonel Gowon was the new leader of what was the same government in Nigeria and that his assumption of power came with the consent of the Supreme Military Council. The Gowon regime had informed the diplomatic corps in Lagos that it did not believe recognition to be an issue. The memorandum gave explicit instructions to the State Department press officer. If the question of recognition of Nigeria was raised, the response was to be along the following lines: "The Embassy in Lagos has been in continual contact with the authorities in Nigeria. Relations between the United States and Nigeria have continued and the question of recognition does not arise."

Togo, 1967. The same position was adopted in reaction to the coup in Togo in January 1967 when the army seized power in a bloodless coup, ousting President Grunitzky. On January 17, the U.S. ambassador advised the department that the situation remained calm with the new government apparently in full and effective control. The new government had announced its intentions to respect all treaties and agreements and to remain faithful to the UN Charter. The ambassador further stated that several governments had shown an intention to conduct normal relations with the new regime. The president of Niger was quoted as saying recognition did not arise since Niger recognized states and not governments. General Soglo of Dahomey announced that the change in regime did not affect relations. A Ghanaian official indicated that the coup had the support of the people and that Ghana would continue normal relations with the new government. Nigeria also announced that it would carry on normal relations with the new regime and would not make any statement concerning recognition. France followed its standard position of recognizing states and not governments. The United Kingdom adopted the same attitude, hoping to avoid the question of recognition. Because of the initiative by African states, the U.S. ambassador requested authority to begin relations with the new government by transmitting a routine diplomatic note from the embassy to the foreign minister announcing the return of the ambassador. The department agreed and authorized the ambassador to resume relations with the new government. No formal act or statement of recognition was given. Diplomatic relations were continued on January 19.

Sierra Leone, 1967. Following a controversial general election in Sierra Leone in which both the ruling Sierra Leone People's Party and the opposition All People's Congress claimed victory, the army stepped in on March 23, 1967, to take over full power in an almost bloodless coup.

A cable to the U.S. embassy underlined the consistency of the American response and the U.S. desire to avoid formal acts of recognition. The department instructed the embassy that, since the government of Sierra Leone had not raised the issue of recognition, the embassy should avoid any reference to recognition as long as possible.

The department press officer was instructed to say, if asked, that the question of recognition did not arise.

The embassy was further instructed that, until the situation became more clear, embassy officials should conduct business as usual on low levels where necessary, but should seek instructions from the department if formal acts (that is, delivery of notes) were required. This was consistent with the current practice, and it gave the department a chance to measure the reaction to the coup in African capitals. Here, as in most other instances of the period, the United States slipped away from early precautionary limitations on normal diplomatic relations and made no announcement of recognition.

Dahomey (Benin), 1967. The United States awaited the lead of France in the December 1967 coup in Dahomey (Benin), in which a group of army officers overthrew the government of President Soglo—the fifth coup d'etat in Dahomey in seven years. The diplomatic corps was informed that provisional President Kouandete wished to receive recognition. The French felt the situation was too unstable to grant recognition. On December 19, the State Department instructed the embassy to avoid any reference to the possible issue of recognition as long as possible. The embassy was instructed to conduct business on an informal basis, but to avoid formal acts, and to inform the department if the new government raised the question of recognition. The department also noted that this procedure avoided the necessity of a formal announcement regarding recognition before the course of events became clear. The department was anxious to assure that treatment of Dahomey did not complicate the issues posed by the coup in Greece and cautioned the embassy not be drawn into public discussions of U.S. recognition policy. Consequently, the United States maintained a low profile and resumed relations, concluding as usual that the question of recognition did not arise.

Three African coups occurred in 1968—in Sierra Leone in April, in Congo-Brazzaville in September, and in Mali in November. In all three, the United States followed its by now established policy and concluded that no question of recognition arose.

Far East

Vietnam, 1963. The first coup in the Far East to confront President Johnson occurred in South Vietnam in November 1963. General Duong Van Minh overthrew the regime of Ngo Dinh Diem in the celebrated takeover that resulted in the death of Diem. This was but the first of a rash of coups to occur in South Vietnam in 1963–1966. However, it was the only coup in which the United States publicly addressed the issue of recognition.

The factors that contributed to U.S. reticence to raise the issue of recognition are readily apparent. The United States in 1963 was substantially involved in the war raging within South Vietnam. By 1966, it was also deeply engaged in the bitter fighting. Under these circumstances, the United States could hardly refuse to recognize a new government, even if it disapproved of the overthrow. The U.S. aim was to minimize the possibility that another state might raise the issue of recognition and then refuse to recognize the new government.

In the initial coup, the United States on November 2 acknowledged receipt of a note requesting recognition from the new regime in South Vietnam. In responding to the note, the department stated, "The Government of the United States shares with the provisional government of the Republic of Vietnam the strong hope that cordial relations between our countries will continue as in the past."[35]

Vietnam, 1964. In January 1964, General Nguyen Khanh, in a bloodless coup, took over as prime minister of the provisional government and chairman of the Revolutionary Military Council. General Minh remained as chief of state.

In a telegram on January 30, the department informed the embassy that the continuation of normal relations was probably the best approach to follow given the circumstances. This approach would avoid difficulties for the government of Vietnam in trying to obtain new acts of recognition from other countries so soon after the November coup. The government of Vietnam might well encounter long delays in obtaining recognition from certain states that had recognized the previous government.

The embassy was instructed to stress to Khanh that the United States could handle the matter as a continuation of relations only if the government of Vietnam approached the United States with a proper note on the recognition issue. The department suggested that in the note the government of Vietnam should indicate that there had been a change in the chairmanship of the Military Council and that the council continued to respect the Republic of Vietnam's international obligations. The department requested that the note make no reference to the question of recognition.[36]

This suggestion was adopted by the government of Vietnam and

---

[35] U.S. Department of State, *Telegram, Washington to Saigon,* November 2, 1963.

[36] U.S. Department of State, *Telegram, Washington to Saigon,* January 30, 1964.

its note to the United States did not mention recognition. The department acknowledged receipt of the Vietnamese note indicating the change in personnel and the willingness of the government to honor its international obligations. This approach was possible since the head of state, General Minh, was not removed by the coup.

Vietnam, 1965. The United States reached the same conclusion when the Vietnamese army overthrew Premier Tran Van Huong in January 1965. The coup was viewed as a rebuff to American efforts to establish a stable civilian government that would press the war against the Viet Cong.

The embassy requested instructions from the department immediately after the coup and indicated that it had not raised the question of recognition of the new regime. In the embassy's view, while the provisional charter of October 20, 1964, was substantially retained and the military seemed to have gone to considerable effort to give their act a flavor of legality and continuity, the chief of state and the prime minister had been removed from office by the action of the armed forces and a new chief of state would be selected from a body different from that set forth in the provisional charter. However, the embassy concluded that this was a case where the United States could raise the question of recognition or not as best suited the policy aims of the United States. Thus, the embassy requested the authority to raise the question of recognition if circumstances looked favorable.

After some delay, the United States concluded that it would be preferable not to raise openly the recognition question, but instead accomplish recognition quietly by proceeding to deal with the new government. Declining to raise the question would, among other things, avoid the problem that concerned the department in the January 1964 coup—the need to obtain recognition from other countries.

Near East

President Johnson faced several irregular changes of government in the Near East. In general, he responded in a low-key manner, and avoided the issue where possible.

In January 1966, the Ba'th government of Syria was overthrown by a group of Ba'th military officers of the radical left. The United States took the position that the new regime was a continuation of the existing government, and that the question of recognition did not arise.

In July 1968, the Iraqi government headed by President Abdul Rahman Arif was overthrown. The United States did not have diplomatic relations at the time and saw no need to consider the question of recognition by the new government.

In at least two other situations—Syria, in October 1968, and Saudi Arabia, in November 1964—arguably irregular changes of government occurred, but since there were elements of continuity, the question of recognition was not raised.

Europe

Greece, 1967. In April 1967 Greek military officers overthrew the government of Prime Minister Kanellopoulos, declared a state of siege, and suspended certain articles of the constitution affecting civil liberties. King Constantine refused to sign the decree imposing the state of siege but did swear in the new government. On December 13 the king tried but failed to overthrow the junta and fled the country. On the same day the junta appointed a regent who in turn appointed a cabinet composed of the leaders of the April coup. The U.S. response to these events was spelled out in a memorandum submitted to the Senate Committee on Foreign Relations:

> The new cabinet justified the rapid political changes on the ground that the King had "abandoned" his duties as monarch, and according to the Constitution, the government had appointed a regent as chief of state. The Department of State, in considering the question of the legitimacy of the new government, examined the 1952 Greek Constitution. The Department concluded that the actions of the junta in appointing a regent and arranging for the appointment of a new Prime Minister were not in conformity with the Constitution, since in the absence of the King from the country, the Parliament (which had been dismissed during the April coup) should have been convened to select a regent. The Department therefore concluded that the regime holding power in Greece on December 14 was an extra-constitutional regime.[37]

Having reached this conclusion, the department instructed the embassy to refrain from formal contact with the new regime, although low-level contact for the purpose of information-gathering could be continued.

In reviewing the situation the department concluded that the

---

[37] Senate Committee on Foreign Relations, *Hearings on S. Res. 205*, pp. 23–24.

new regime was in control of the country; that the king's attempted coup had failed; and that the new regime had announced its intention to promulgate a new constitution and hold elections. In addition, several NATO countries had informed the United States that they would soon regularize their relations with the new government. On January 23, 1968, the U.S. ambassador to Greece was authorized to pay an official call on Foreign Minister Pipinelis.[38]

Did this action constitute recognition of the new Greek government? The memorandum submitted to the Foreign Relations Committee by the Department of State evades the question:

> In a press briefing on January 23, 1968, the Department's spokesman was asked about the significance of Ambassador Talbot's visit with the Foreign Minister. He answered that "we now have normal diplomatic contacts with the Government of Greece." The spokesman was then asked whether "the fact of normal diplomatic contacts means that we now recognize that there has been no change in the constitutional structure and the head of state remains the same." The spokesman further said that "the United States Government continues to regard King Constantine as the chief of state of Greece. Relations between the King and the Government—the Government in Athens—are an internal Greek matter not properly a subject for comment by the United States Government." A member of the press asked whether our Ambassador was accredited to the Government of Athens. The spokesman replied that "the Ambassador and other American diplomats are accredited to the King. We consider the Government in Athens to be the Government of Greece."[39]

Czechoslovakia, 1968. In early 1968, under intense pressure from the Soviet Union, Alexander Dubcek resigned his post as party first secretary in Czechoslovakia. This was followed by the resignation of Antonin Novotny as president. General Ludvik Svoboda replaced Novotny as president of Czechoslovakia.

The question of recognition was raised internally within the U.S. government on this occasion. On August 26, the Department of State instructed the U.S. mission to NATO to seek agreement in principle that member governments would discuss problems privately before taking any action that might constitute recognition of the new Czechoslovakian government. The department noted that practical difficulties

---

[38] Ibid.
[39] Ibid., p. 24.

would arise if governments sought to withhold recognition while maintaining a presence in Prague.[40] On August 27 the United Kingdom indicated that it was waiting to hear what Svoboda said on August 28. If he indicated that his government essentially remained in office, the foreign office was prepared to say that the question of recognition did not arise. France agreed that recognition was not an issue.

On August 28, the State Department indicated that its attitude would depend on what kind of regime was installed. If a quisling regime was imposed, recognition would be an issue. The department noted that legal doctrine gave it considerable leeway.[41] However, the United Kingdom informed the United States that since under the Czech constitution a government endorsed by the president was the constitutional government, it was satisfied that the question of recognition did not arise. The United States, by not taking any formal action, adopted this position also.[42]

Conclusion

The Johnson administration's recognition policy toward Latin America is more difficult to categorize than the Kennedy policy. Clearly, the commitment to a return to constitutional government as a condition to the grant of recognition did not receive as much emphasis under Johnson, as Table 2 reflects. Interest in a return to constitutional government did not vanish, however. The United States inquired about a regime's intent to restore constitutional government through the medium of free elections in the 1964 coup in Bolivia, the 1966 coup in Argentina, and the 1968 coups in Peru and Panama. In none of these instances did the United States obtain an election timetable; instead it settled for vague promises to hold elections sometime in the future. In short, Johnson reconciled the "often conflicting goals of anti-Communism, non-involvement in domestic politics, and discouraging the overthrow of constitutionally elected regimes" in a different way than President Kennedy, weighing the goal of anti-communism more heavily than the goal of discouraging the overthrow of constitutionally elected governments.[43] Underlying this approach was the judgment of most Johnson advisers that the United States could do little to discourage such coups.

---

[40] U.S. Department of State, Telegram, Washington to Brussels, August 26, 1968.

[41] U.S. Department of State, Telegram, Washington to Brussels, August 28, 1968.

[42] Maher, "Kennedy and Johnson Responses," p. 198. For a breakdown of the criteria relied upon in the public announcement of recognition during the presidency of Lyndon Johnson, see Appendix B.

[43] Maher, "Kennedy and Johnson Responses," p. 193.

Table 2

TIME SPANS BETWEEN LATIN AMERICAN COUPS D'ETAT,
U.S. RECOGNITION, AND NEXT ELECTION IN COUP STATES,
1963–1968

Country	Coup d'Etat	U.S. Recognition	Time Span between Coup and Recognition (days)	Election	Time Span between Coup and Election
Brazil	April 1, 1964	Suspension of diplomatic relations deemed unnecessary	—	April 11, 1964	10 days
Bolivia	Nov. 4, 1964	Dec. 8, 1964	34	July 3, 1966	1 yr., 7 mos., 30 days
Argentina	June 28, 1966	July 15, 1966	17	—	—
Peru	Oct 3, 1968	Oct. 25, 1968	22	—	—
Panama	Oct. 11, 1968	Nov. 13, 1968	33	—	—
			Average 26.5		

Source: Maher, "Kennedy and Johnson Responses," p. 198.

The milder recognition response of Johnson to coups d'etat in Latin America was a harbinger of the virtually automatic recognition response of President Nixon to such coups. President Johnson was still concerned with obtaining a commitment to a return to constitutional government but he was not willing to risk as much as Kennedy to obtain the commitment.

The United States did move under Johnson to an automatic recognition policy toward Africa that differed in practice very little from the Estrada Doctrine. Numerous coups by the military occurred in Africa during the Johnson presidency. The U.S. response usually was simply to resume relations in as quiet and inconspicuous a manner as possible. Deemphasizing recognition to the point of eliminating the concept altogether served this purpose. This low-profile policy at times fell into confusing semantic and conceptual difficulties, but as a practical matter, proved very effective. In other parts of the world, the United States responded to coups in an ad hoc manner, with the recognition action determined by the regional political forces.

Recognition policy under Johnson was in a transitory phase. The emphasis on and use of recognition as a bargaining tool to obtain a commitment to a return to constitutional government in Latin America was receding, but remained a factor in U.S. practice. In Africa, the transition was made from the use of recognition as a passive political instrument to a virtually automatic policy of resuming relations with whatever regime was in power, and avoiding the use of even the term *recognition*. It remained for President Nixon to extend this policy to the rest of the world.

4

U.S. RECOGNITION POLICY UNDER RICHARD NIXON AND GERALD FORD, 1969-1976

The evolution of recognition policy toward the "usual" military coup d'etat continued during the presidency of Richard Nixon. In certain instances, however, especially where the United States suffered significant political reversals and where it opposed the new government that came to power out of these reversals, recognition was withheld. The most notable instances were the fall of South Vietnam and Cambodia in 1975 and the civil war in Angola in 1975–1976. In the usual case recognition was increasingly deemphasized and downgraded to the point of nonexistence. The only notable policy shift toward the typical military coup was the abandonment of the earlier practice of officially suspending diplomatic relations whenever an extraconstitutional change of government occurred. This change was simply another step in the process of deemphasizing recognition.

Cranston Resolution

In 1969, the first year of the Nixon presidency, the Senate passed Resolution 205 which set forth the sense of the Senate that the recognition of a foreign government did not imply that the United States necessarily approved of the form, ideology, or policy of that foreign government. The resolution, which was sponsored by Senator Cranston (Democrat, California), had the support of the Department of State.[1]

The resolution was designed, according to Senator Cranston, to dispel the confusion "about what United States recognition of a

---

[1] U.S. Congress, Senate, Committee on Foreign Relations, S. Report 91-338, 91st Cong., 1st sess. (1969).

EXTRACONSTITUTIONAL CHANGES OF GOVERNMENT IN FOREIGN STATES DURING PRESIDENCIES OF RICHARD M. NIXON AND GERALD R. FORD

Latin America

1. *Bolivia, September 1969.* Military coup ousted President Siles Salinas. Alfredo Ovando proclaimed president.
2. *Brazil, August-October 1969.* President Artur da Costa e Silva suffered a stroke and three-man military junta assumed power, not permitting the vice-president to succeed to the presidency. Costa e Silva died on October 7, and the junta chose Emilio Garrastazu Medici to replace him.
3. *Argentina, June 1970.* President Ongania forced to resign and a junta of commanders-in-chief assumed power.
4. *Bolivia, October 1970.* President Alfredo Ovando forced from office by military.
5. *Argentina, March 1971.* Military coup, forcing the resignation of President Livingston.
6. *Bolivia, August 1971.* Right-wing General Hugo Banzer overthrew President Torres, who had himself been installed by military coup.
7. *Ecuador, February 1972.* Overthrow of President Velasco Ibarra by military junta.
8. *Honduras, December 1972.* Overthrow of President Ernesto Cruz by military.
9. *Chile, September 1973.* Overthrow and killing of Salvador Allende.
10. *Honduras, April 1975.* Military overthrow of President Oswaldo Lopez Arellano.
11. *Peru, August 1975.* Overthrow by military of President Velasco Alvarado.
12. *Argentina, March 1976.* Overthrow by military of President Isabel Peron.
13. *Uruguay, June 1976.* Military ouster of President Juan M. Bordaberry.

Africa

14. *Libya, September 1969.* Monarchy overthrown and Revolutionary Command Council established.
15. *Somalia, October 1969.* Somalian army backed by police seized power from civilian government.
16. *Dahomey, December 1969.* Lieutenant Colonel Kouandete overthrew seventeen-month-old regime of Dr. Zinsou.
17. *Lesotho, June 1970.* Chief Jonathan assumed full power and suspended the constitution.
18. *Uganda, January 1971.* President Milton Obote ousted by army.
19. *Ghana, January 1972.* Army seized power, ousting Prime Minister Busia.

20. *Swaziland, April 1973.* Constitutional monarch scrapped the constitution and assumed full power.
21. *Rwanda, July 1973.* Army overthrew president after months of tribal unrest.
22. *Upper Volta, February 1974.* General Lamizana led army coup. Army took over government and dissolved parliament.
23. *Niger, April 1974.* Military coup overthrew President Diori.
24. *Ethiopia, September 1974.* Army ousted Emperor Haile Selassie in a bloodless coup.
25. *Chad, April 1975.* Military coup.
26. *Malagasy Republic, June 1975.* Military coup.
27. *Nigeria, July 1975.* Overthrow of President Gowon.
28. *Angola, November 1975-February 1976.* The civil war over control of new state in which the Popular Movement for the Liberation of Angola emerged victorious.
29. *Nigeria, March 1976.* Overthrow of General Mohammed Murtala by military officers.

Asia

30. *Pakistan, March 1969.* Field Marshal Ayub Khan resigned the presidency after five months of violent civil demonstrations against his regime. General Agha Mohammad Yahya Khan, the commander in chief of the army, imposed martial law at Ayub's request and proclaimed himself president five days later.
31. *Afghanistan, July 1974.* King overthrown by his brother-in-law.
32. *Bangladesh, August 1975.* Armed forces overthrew and killed President Mujibur Rahman.
33. *Cambodia, March 1975.* Khmer Rouge overturned temporary government which replaced government of Lon Nol.
34. *South Vietnam, April 1975.* Government of President Thieu collapsed under communist pressure.
35. *Bangladesh, November 1975.* Bangladesh army leadership took control of country from the junior officers who seized power in August, 1975.

Other Parts of the World

36. *Portugal, April 1974.* Army overthrew Premier Marcelo Caetans.
37. *Lebanon, March 1976.* Military seizure of power in midst of civil war.

---

foreign government really means today." It dealt only with the implications or consequences of recognition and did not set forth any criteria or conditions for determining when recognition should be accorded.

The resolution coincided with the trend in the department to deemphasize recognition, and the desire to deemphasize recognition is fully consistent with the Cranston Resolution. However, the resolution had little influence on policy because it was purely hortatory and did not address the central issue of what criteria should be used in deciding when to accord recognition. Consequently, no mention was made of the Cranston Resolution in cases where there was substantial domestic sentiment to withhold recognition, for example, on the assumption of power by the Communists in South Vietnam in 1975.

Latin America

Bolivia, 1969. The United States moved away from its practice of formally suspending relations upon an extraconstitutional change of government in the September 1969 military overthrow of President Louis Adolpho Siles Salinas of Bolivia.[2]

The United States received a note dated September 27 stating that the new Bolivian government wished to continue to strengthen the friendly relations between Bolivia and the United States. The new government informed the United States that it exercised full authority throughout the country, enjoyed the support of the people, and would maintain and honor Bolivia's international obligations and continue the international policy of firm adhesion to principles that sustained the international community.

On October 10 the United States delivered a note to the Bolivian foreign minister indicating the continuance of diplomatic relations. The note did not mention recognition; it merely stated the desire of the United States to continue and to improve the friendly relations which existed between the two countries. The new Bolivian government made no firm commitment to hold elections. Despite this, the United States extended recognition, at least implicitly, through the note indicating continuance of relations.

In a break with past practice, the United States did not publicly state that the overthrow of the government automatically suspended diplomatic relations, as it had in the coups in Panama and Peru the previous year. Nor was this change a result of oversight. The Department of State attempted to evade the question of formal suspension

---

[2] This change in policy came one week after the Cranston Resolution was adopted by the Senate. Thus, it seems safe to assume that in the Bolivian situation, the United States was attempting to avoid any implication that recognition of the government of Bolivia implied approval by moving away from the use of recognition as a lever to extract commitments on matters covered by Resolution XXVI, such as free elections and the protection of human rights.

of relations in a further effort to downgrade the concept of recognition of foreign governments. Under this approach, the concern for constitutional government and democracy was to be reflected in the character of continuing U.S. relations with the countries rather than in the recognition of their governments.

In handling press questions, the press officer stated that the United States neither denied nor confirmed that the relations with Bolivia were suspended or broken. In his words, the United States did not characterize the nature of relations with Bolivia other than to say, "We were assessing developments closely." The press then asked whether relations were ever suspended or broken during the days following the coup. The reply: "There was a temporary period in which we reviewed the facts and determined whether we would maintain normal diplomatic relations."[3]

Most Latin American states also announced continuance of relations within two or three weeks after the coup. When the United States acted on October 10, a number of Latin American states, including Brazil, Uruguay, Argentina, and Peru, had already recognized or resumed relations with Bolivia.

There was a further change in the U.S. approach to the Bolivian coup. In the Peruvian and Panamanian coups of October 1968, the United States had made formal inquiry of the new regimes' intentions with regard to points covered by paragraph 2(a) and (b) of Resolution XXVI in business letters addressed to the general designated as foreign minister. However, in the Bolivian case, because of the change of policy, a direct oral approach instead of a letter was used to obtain a statement of the regime's general direction and attitude toward relations with the United States.

The last military coups during the presidency of President Johnson and the first under President Nixon did not allow the United States to apply its other method of deemphasizing recognition—"no question of recognition arises"—because few, if any, elements of continuity existed between the deposed governments and the new regimes. However, beginning with the extraconstitutional change of government in Brazil in September 1969, the United States found enough elements of continuity in the next four military coups in Latin America to conclude that the question of recognition did not arise.

Brazil, 1969. On August 31, 1969, President Artur da Costa e Silva suffered a stroke and a three-man military junta assumed control of the government, purporting to have the president's consent. The junta's

---

[3] U.S. Department of State, *Press Conference*, October 10, 1969.

official statement declared that the political situation did not permit the vice-president, Costa e Silva's rightful successor under the constitution, to assume the presidency. The junta pledged to continue Costa e Silva's program and to uphold the constitution while temporarily ruling the country until a new president could be chosen. Costa e Silva died on October 7 and the junta chose General Medici to replace him, stressing the continuity between the two presidents in its prepared statement. There were student demonstrations during these events but no reported violence.

The question of recognition could have arisen here in two ways. First there was a question of recognition of the three-man junta that took over on August 31. The United States, however, following its policy of downplaying the recognition question, took the position that no question of recognition arose since the accession to power was only temporary in order to provide continuity in government. The press spokesman for the department expanded upon this position on September 2:

> The question of recognition does not appear to arise with the United States in the current circumstances. It would appear that the effect of the Institutional Act, No. 12 [statutory act to provide continuity in leadership] is to provide administrative continuity for a temporary period during the incapacity of the President. And again it would appear that the Institutional Act envisions that the President will resume full exercise of his functions.[4]

When Costa e Silva died on October 7 and the junta chose General Medici to replace him, the United States again concluded that no question of recognition arose. During this period, the U.S. government approach to recognition of Latin American regimes was in transition toward the goal of making recognition almost automatic in accord with the Estrada Doctrine. Consequently, in implementing this policy, it served U.S. interests to conclude that the question of recognition did not arise in cases where there were elements of continuity between the old and new governments. Here the United States accepted the Brazilian government's thesis that the change of government was a normal succession under the military rule and the series of institutional acts that had been the essence of the Brazilian government since 1964.

Argentina, 1970. The United States followed much the same approach in the June 9, 1970, change of government in Argentina when Presi-

---

[4] Ibid., September 2, 1969.

dent Ongania was forced to resign, and the junta of commanders-in-chief assumed power. The Argentine minister of foreign affairs stated that the change in the leadership of the government took place within the framework of the Statute of the Argentine Revolution and that a new president would be designated in ten days. Most members of the previous cabinet remained in office, and business throughout the country proceeded as usual. On June 13, General Roberto Marcel Livingston was named president by the junta.

On June 10, the U.S. embassy in Buenos Aires received a note from the Argentine minister of foreign affairs informing it of the change in government and indicating that the change in leadership took place within the framework of the Statute of Argentine Revolution. In acknowledging receipt of the note the Department of State indicated that it had concluded that the change of leadership did not give rise to a question of recognition since there had been no basic discontinuity in the military government of Argentina.

The United States also took the position that consultations under Resolution XXVI were not called for when no question of recognition arose. The United States consulted informally with several governments but did not invoke Resolution XXVI.

Chile, Uruguay, and Honduras, among others, agreed that the issue of recognition did not arise as a result of the change in leadership. Bolivia stated that relations with the government of Argentina would not be affected. Brazil also avoided the recognition problem. Japan and Great Britain, among non-Western hemisphere countries, also accepted the thesis that there was continuity between the old and new regimes.

Bolivia, 1970. The "no question of recognition arises" formula was used again five months later in the forced resignation of President Alfredo Ovando of Bolivia. On October 10, the Bolivian government delivered a note to the U.S. embassy informing it of the change in government. The note stated that Juan Jose Torres Gonzales had assumed leadership by mandate of the armed forces, labor classes, and the university, and that the government had complete control and authority over all the territory of the republic as well as the support of Bolivian people of all classes. The note continued that the government would maintain and fulfill international obligations and stated the desire of the government to continue and improve the relations between Bolivia and the United States. On October 12 the department acknowledged the note of October 10 from the new government of Bolivia. Recognition was not mentioned.

At the noon press briefing on October 13, the press officer reported that the United States had replied to the Bolivian note and that relations were continuing. The officer stated that the assumption of leadership of the revolutionary government by Torres was with the acquiescence of the same military institutions that had supported Ovando, who had been overthrown. Thus, the Torres government was a continuation of the Ovando government since it rested on the same mandate from the armed forces. Military institutions continued governing under Torres as they had under Ovando. In the department's view, Resolution XXVI consultations were not called for since the question of recognition did not arise because of the continuity in government.[5]

Argentina, 1971. The United States adopted the same policy for the fourth time following the assumption of power by the commanders-in-chief of the armed forces in Argentina in March 1971. The junta forced the resignation of President Livingston and assumed the executive power of the state.

The State Department took the position that this situation was basically the same as the one in June 1970 and that no question of recognition arose. The 1970 decision had been based on a legal interpretation that residual power of the revolutionary government rested with the junta. Consequently, the department's position was that the change of leadership did not give rise to a question of recognition since there was no basic discontinuity in the military government of Argentina.

In a press briefing on March 25, the press officer referred to the exchange of notes and indicated that there was basic continuity in the military government and that normal relations were continuing. Various other Latin American countries, such as Brazil and Panama, quickly took the same position.[6] On March 25, the United States acknowledged the note from the new Argentine government indicating the change in leadership. The U.S. reply did not mention recognition or resumption of relations.

Bolivia, 1971. The United States, although finding no elements of continuity in the August 19, 1971, overthrow of President Torres in Bolivia by right-wing General Hugo Banzer, announced that it would continue relations with the new regime on August 31.

The U.S. embassy received a note from the new government of

---

[5] Ibid., October 13, 1969.

[6] In this instance Venezuela, which normally refused to recognize any government that came to power in violation of the domestic law of the state, agreed that there had been no unconstitutional change of government in Argentina.

Bolivia on August 24, informing it of the recent change of government. On August 23, the State Department had announced that it was studying developments in Bolivia but declined to comment on the possibility of recognition of the new government.[7] The note received from the Bolivian government informed the United States of the make-up of the new government and stated that the new government would respect international obligations. Mexico announced that it would as usual follow the Estrada Doctrine. Under this doctrine, Mexico would watch events in Bolivia closely while continuing relations. Guatemala also announced that it would apply the Estrada Doctrine. Argentina announced on August 25 that diplomatic relations would continue.

After informal consultations with a number of Latin American countries, on August 31 the United States acknowledged the note from Bolivia and indicated that it was happy to continue relations.

The press officer, when questioned, did state that the continuation of relations constituted implicit recognition of the new regime.[8] Although the U.S. note to the new regime used the words *continuing relations,* the press officer stated the United States considered that the question of recognition arose in this case. A number of reporters pursued the problems of recognition at some length. The interplay between the press officer and the reporters brought out the change in recognition policy that had occurred.

> Q. For some time on these cases, the phrase—the question of recognition does not arise—was used. Does this have any significance—the fact that you handled this one somewhat differently in your announcement?
>
> A. Not materially. If the question is: Does this mean that we are recognizing the Government of Bolivia? The answer is that it is implicit in the continuance of relations, which is the substance of what I have said about our note.
>
> Q. Well, this is diplomatic hair-splitting but it can be important. When the question of recognition doesn't arise, presumably, things are just continued. Do you consider that in using the phraseology that you have today that there was a period in which there was no recognition?
>
> A. Let me try it this way—each case depends on the circumstances. In this case there are fewer elements of continuity than when the Torres government succeeded the Ovando government. In contrast with that case, this new government does not assert continuity with its predeces-

---

[7] U.S. Department of State, *For the Press,* August 24, 1971.

[8] U.S. Department of State, *Press Conference,* August 31, 1971.

sor. However, I should point out that there is continuity in U.S. policy.

In each of the three coups d'etat in Bolivia since the death of President Barrientos, we have focused on the question of diplomatic relations with the new Government, and in each case decided to continue those relations with the Government effectively in power.

Q. Is this, then, equivalent to our extending diplomatic recognition to a new government, or do we see this as simply one of continued recognition despite three unconstitutional overthrows of the preceding government?

A. You can't get away from the fact that there is a new Government, so that the answer to your first question is a direct Yes—that this is direct recognition of the new Government.

Q. What accounts for the period of time that passed before this decision was made?

A. On background—The first most important consideration was for the U.S. Government to receive some notification from the Government of its intentions with respect to international affairs, its desire to have relations with the U.S. Government, and to ascertain that it was, at least in present circumstances, in effective control of the government. The note was not received here until August the 23rd, so that while each of these situations may differ in some degree, the delay has not been an extended one.

Q. A week passed between the time that note was received, and this announcement was made. Is that a normal period of time for this sort of thing?

A. Roughly, the average period.

Q. Does this come in concert with similar or identical actions by other members of the OAS?

A. I don't have a list of the other governments who have recognized, but among them are several OAS countries. I think that perhaps one important thing relevant here is the policy statement of the President in October 1969, wherein he expressed the principle on behalf of this present administration, his administration, to deal with governments as they are in Latin America.

Q. What you're saying in effect is that we're going through a metamorphosis in our process of recognizing, shying away from the old process of continuity and accepting then the de facto and not necessarily the de jure?

A. I think that observation is valid with respect to Latin America. It is within that framework that the policy of 1969 was spelled out. Now, we have a different situation in another part of the world.

Q. In this policy toward Latin America governments, have we abandoned one of the former criteria—which was their declaration of willingness to assume the international obligations in respect to the treaty, et cetera, of their predecessors?

A. No, no. That would be a consideration in higher action.

Q. Now, when did they do this? Or was this in their note or was it done in consultations with them down there?

A. I am advised it was in their note.[9]

The press officer in response to a question indicated that the United States was going through a "metamorphosis" in which it was moving toward acceptance of de facto regimes as they existed, at least in Latin America.[10] Further, the press officer underlined the U.S. focus on diplomatic relations and the continuity of those relations with the new government. He did concede, however, that recognition was "implicit" in the continuance of diplomatic relations. At no point did he concede that relations were ever suspended as a result of a change of government.

Ecuador, 1972. The continuation of relations formula was applied again in the February 1972 overthrow of President Velasco Ibarra of Ecuador by a military junta considered moderate and pro-Western. On February 22, the United States delivered a note to the Ecuadorean foreign office responding to Ecuador's note of February 17 advising the United States of a change in the government. The U.S. note stated that the United States wished to maintain friendly relations with the government of Ecuador.[11] The word *recognition* was not mentioned.

A number of other countries had already acted by February 23. Bolivia announced on February 19 that it would continue diplomatic relations with the government of Ecuador, as Venezuela did on February 26. The government of Uruguay acknowledged the Ecuadorean note on February 22. The government of Brazil officially recognized the new Ecuadorean government on February 21. On February 22, the government of Chile affirmed its desire to continue existing relations with Ecuador, as Panama had on February 17. Peru and Argentina also announced that they would continue relations with the new regime.

Other Latin American Coups. Six successful coups have occurred in Latin America since February 1972: (1) The December 1972 over-

---

[9] Ibid.

[10] Ibid.

[11] Department of State, *U.S. Policy toward Latin America*, p. 103.

throw of President Ernesto Cruz of Honduras; (2) the September 19, 1973, overthrow of Salvador Allende of Chile;[12] (3) the April 22, 1975, removal of President Oswaldo Lopez Arellano in Honduras; (4) the August 29, 1975, overthrow of President Velasco Alvarado of Peru;[13] (5) the March 24, 1976, overthrow of President Isabel Peron of Argentina;[14] and (6) the June 12, 1976, overthrow of President Juan Bordaberry of Uruguay. Generally, in each coup the United States continued its policy of deemphasizing recognition and simply continuing relations after the major Latin American states had officially acted.

Africa

Libya, 1969. The United States reemphasized the recognition process somewhat in the September 1969 military coup d'etat in Libya. On September 2, the armed forces seized power and proclaimed Libya a Socialist republic. Twenty-four hours after the coup, several countries recognized the new regime—the United Arab Republic, Sudan, Algeria, and South Yemen. East Germany also quickly extended

---

[12] On September 11, 1973, the armed forces overthrew the government of President Salvador Allende Gossens and established a four-man military junta to govern the country. The Department of State informed the embassy in Santiago that it had been moving away from its traditional policy of recognition which many people believed signified U.S. approval of a new government. Although the United States had not adopted the Estrada Doctrine, it merely informed a new government of its intention to continue formal diplomatic relations after it was clear that the new government was in effective control and after other states had taken similar action.

Following this policy, on September 24, after twenty-nine states had recognized the new government, the U.S. ambassador to Chile delivered a note to the Chilean foreign minister indicating the U.S. desire to continue relations. Department of State, *U.S. Policy toward Latin America*, p. 34.

[13] On August 29, 1975, a military junta in Peru deposed President Juan Velasco Alvarado in a bloodless coup. The junta, led by Gen. Francisco Morales Bermudez, evidently acted as a result of Velasco's failing health and his order exiling twenty-nine persons, mainly of leftist persuasion. While the State Department took no official position, American officials in Peru favored the change of government. On August 30, in response to questions from the press, the department spokesman stated that the question of recognition did not arise and that the department expected the ambassador to deal with the new regime.

[14] President Isabel Peron, who ascended to the presidency of Argentina in 1974 following the death of her husband, Juan Peron, was overthrown by the military in a long-awaited coup d'etat on June 24, 1975. On June 25, the Department of State announced that relations with Argentina would be unchanged as a result of the change of government. According to the department, this announcement amounted to de facto recognition of the new military government. UPI reported that the U.S. government was informed of the coup in advance and raised no objection, except to oppose a bloody takeover like that in Chile the previous year. *Washington Post*, March 25, 1976, p. A21.

recognition. Libya's new military regime on September 2 reassured the United States and other Western nations that it would honor all agreements, including those relating to the American Wheelus Air Force Base and vast oil concessions. On September 3, Colonel Sharib summoned foreign diplomats to a meeting and formally notified them that he regarded their presence as de facto recognition of his regime by their governments. He indicated again to the diplomats that Libya would respect all its international commitments.

Great Britain, the United States, and France extended recognition to the new Libyan regime on September 6. France and Libya exchanged messages stating their desire to maintain and develop friendly relations. A ministry spokesman in Paris said that this constituted diplomatic recognition. In Washington officials publicly said that U.S. recognition was being extended to the regime whose leadership, composition, and direction were still little known.

In announcing that diplomatic relations were being maintained with the Libyan regime, the spokesman for the Department of State was authorized to comment in response to a question on the recognition of Libya as follows:

> The United States Government has noted the statement of the Revolutionary Command Council that all nations maintaining diplomatic relations with Libya are considered as recognizing the new Libyan Government. The United States has maintained diplomatic relations with the Government of Libya and looks forward to a continuation of traditionally close ties between our two countries.[15]

The department spokesman could say, if asked, that this action amounted to recognition. On background, the department spokesman was authorized to say that in reaching this decision to maintain diplomatic relations, the United States had taken into consideration the assurances that Libya would respect all international agreements and treaties and observe the rights of petroleum companies there.

For background information the press officers were given guidance on the question: Is our action consistent with past policy and precedent? The drafted answer to this question sets out basic U.S. policy:

> Generally speaking, our practice regarding the continuance of diplomatic relations in cases where governments have been changed by military coups is first to study the situation

---

[15] *New York Times*, September 7, 1969, cited in J. Wadlow, "Recent U.S. Recognition Policy toward Coups d'Etat," unpublished manuscript (on file with author), p. 3.

and inform ourselves of what is taking place. The United States Government is interested in many aspects of the situation; for example, whether the new government appeared in effective control of the territory and in possession of the administrative machinery of state; whether the new government had the general acquiescence of the population, and whether the new regime has indicated its intent to carry out its international obligations. While the facts are coming in, we usually seek to maintain contact with the local government. Our course of action in Libya has been in accord with our continuance of normal diplomatic relations following other recent changes in government. For example, coups occurred in Mali—1968, Ghana—1966, Nigeria—January 1966, Burundi—August 1966, Central African Republic—1966, and Congo—1965, to mention only a few. The maintenance of normal diplomatic relations in such circumstances amounts to recognition of the new government.

Question: Does our maintenance of normal diplomatic relations mean that the new government is recognized by the United States?

Answer: Yes. On September the 7th North Vietnam, Poland, Yugoslavia, Iran, Morocco, and Italy announced their recognition. India considered the recent events in Libya as purely of an internal nature and not affecting the relations between the two countries.[16]

The American embassy, in communications with the department, had urged quick recognition. The embassy noted that the junta was in control of the country and that it had agreed to abide by all international agreements, including oral agreements. The embassy argued that the substantial American interest in the country required that the United States deal with whatever regime was in power. The embassy also felt that if there were a prolonged delay in extending formal recognition this would dilute the favorable impression that the hands-off U.S. attitude toward the coup had caused in Libya.

Somalia, 1969. In October 1969, military officers seized power from the elected civilian government one week after the assassination of President Abdirashid Ali Shermarke. The United States concluded that the question of recognition did not arise.

Dahomey (Benin), 1969. The policy followed in Libya and Somalia of handling military coups in a pragmatic and low-key manner continued in the December 1969 coup in Dahomey. The U.S. response is worthy of note because the department gave standby guidance on the problem

---

16 Ibid.

of continuing diplomatic relations after a coup. These instructions illustrate how the U.S. policy on recognition is implemented in the early stages of a coup:

Following is a general standby guidance on problem continuance diplomatic relations with the Government installed by coup and intended for Embassy as applicable:

a) Department hopes question continuance diplomatic relations can be handled in same low-key as in other such situations in Dahomey and as followed by U.S. in other African changes of Government.

b) Embassy should avoid reference to recognition issue and not be drawn into any statements suggesting recognition is major question we shall formally determine and announce.

c) While situation is under study Embassy should keep low-profile to avoid taking sides, maintain working contacts and hold open lines for communication to government officials on informal basis. Position aloofness leaves options open including possibility of exercising limited influence favorable to our interests if and when opportunity presents. If any formal acts, such as delivery of notes, required, Embassy should seek Department instructions.

d) Embassy should report all relevant facts, including control of country, acquiescence of people, government's respect for rule of law, rights of foreign nations and diplomatic missions, and willingness to honor international obligations. It [is] anticipated through increasingly normal routine transactions of business and exchanges of information, Embassy should move toward gradual full resumption of normal diplomatic relations. Embassy shall not precede French and other African governments. Once this point reached, we would acknowledge, if queried, that we recognize new government but would not identify particular act or moment of recognition.[17]

On December 24 the department indicated that it hoped relations with the new regime in Dahomey could be continued in the same low-key, pragmatic way as in Somalia and Libya. The embassy was instructed to continue routine contact, facilitating the return to normal diplomatic relations. The new government of Dahomey had stated that it would honor its international agreements and had demonstrated effective control over the country.

The department authorized the embassy in its discretion to make clear on the appropriate occasion that the U.S. government considered normal diplomatic relations to continue with the new government.

[17] U.S. Department of State, *Telegram, Washington to Cotonou*, December 1966.

The embassy was instructed to avoid a public announcement of recognition. If specifically asked whether the United States recognized the new government, the embassy was authorized to reply in the affirmative without identifying any particular act or moment of recognition.

Lesotho, 1970. In January 1970, Chief Jonathan, the elected head of the government of Lesotho, assumed full power of the government and suspended the constitution. In a telegram to all American embassies in Africa, the department stated that there was no requirement for a public statement on the U.S. government attitude toward continuation of relations with the government of Lesotho, and that it hoped none would eventuate. The department further noted that limitations on holding contacts to the working level were no longer needed and were thus lifted. The department planned to meet any possible press inquiries about Lesotho by saying that the U.S. government had normal relations with the government of Lesotho and continued to have concern for its development and prosperity. This was affirmed by the secretary in a statement on March 26.[18]

Uganda, 1971. A major coup occurred in Uganda in 1971 when the Ugandan army on January 25 ousted President Milton Obote after twelve hours of bloody fighting between rival factions of the armed forces. The United States stated its preliminary position informally on January 26, taking, as in similar cases in the past, a low-key approach with a view to avoiding any formal or dramatic statement of recognition. The embassy would continue to maintain routine working contacts and would keep lines of communication open for government offices. The United States would not, however, conclude any new agreement nor take any other similar actions that would give the appearance of formal recognition. Subsequently, depending upon developments, the United States would move gradually in the direction of fully normal diplomatic relations. When the time was ripe the post would indicate the U.S. government's view that normal diplomatic relations continued.[19]

This is in fact what occurred. The Department of State first, however, awaited an African initiative because of the political problems caused by the change of government. On the one hand, the United States did not want to appear overeager and compromise the

---

[18] U.S. Department of State, *Press Statement by Secretary of State Rogers*, March 26, 1970.

[19] U.S. Department of State, *Telegram from Washington to Kampala*, January 26, 1971.

new regime by quick action; on the other hand, it did not want states such as Tanzania or Zambia, which supported President Milton Obote, to misinterpret the U.S. position as opposition to the Amin regime. Neither did the United States want to isolate the United Kingdom, which had come out strongly for the new regime.

However, because of the actions of other states, by February 12 the United States was well on its way toward resumption of full relations with the Amin government. This was communicated to the United Kingdom and to the American embassies in Africa.

In the meantime, contact was stepped up with the new regime. On February 17 the department instructed the embassy to strengthen further informal contacts. However, the department still wished to delay formal public action such as signing agreements that might be publicly interpreted in a manner that could prejudice African acceptance of the new Ugandan government. The department was encouraged by evidence that, with the exception of Tanzania, the countries initially most active in backing Obote now appeared to be moving more cautiously. The State Department felt that moderate African states, such as the Congo, Ethiopia, and Kenya, would be more effective in fostering acceptance of the new regime if it were not too closely identified with non-African powers. Therefore, the United States avoided formal actions on the eve of the February 26 OAU ministerial meeting in Addis Ababa. This position was communicated informally and unofficially to the new regime in Uganda.[20]

On April 26, in a telegram to the embassy, the department stated that U.S.-Ugandan relations were now on a fully normal basis. If questions were raised, the department indicated that it would respond that relations were now normal. However, the department wished to avoid public comment if possible. A bilateral agreement was to be signed within the next few days, and the department instructed the embassy to limit remarks on the signing of the treaty and not to get into recognition questions. If a question should be raised whether or not a bilateral treaty indicated U.S. recognition, the embassy was instructed to respond that diplomatic relations were now proceeding in a fully normal way. The department instructed the embassy, even if pressed, to avoid the use of recognition or appearing to link recognition with specific actions, such as signing bilateral treaties. If pressed still further, the department instructed the embassy to respond affirmatively without identifying any act or time.[21]

---

[20] U.S. Department of State, *Telegram from Washington to Kampala*, February 17, 1971.

[21] U.S. Department of State, *Telegram from Washington to Kampala*, April 26, 1971.

Ghana, 1972. A coup in Ghana in January 1972 placed pressure on the usual U.S. normalization pattern. Here an army-civilian coalition seized power in a bloodless coup on January 13, ousting Prime Minister Busia. The department wished to avoid making a statement in the hope that African states would accord recognition or normalize relations in a short time. The embassy was instructed to say, if asked, that it was following with interest the installation of new governmental machinery and had noted the government statement. The department informed the embassy that it would respond similarly if asked at the press briefing on January 28.[22]

On January 29 the embassy reported that the new regime was moving toward firmer control of the actual governmental process. In the embassy's view, this development, coupled with the United Kingdom's decision, moved the United States to the threshold of recognition.[23] On January 29 also, in a telegram to the embassy, the department noted that its soundings in Washington indicated that most countries represented in Accra would acquiesce in the government of Ghana's announcement and hence all would normalize relations by January 31. In keeping with the usual practice, the embassy maintained low-level contacts and gradually increased them, until relations were fully normal.[24]

Other African Coups. Since January 1972, several coups have occurred in Africa: (1) Nigeria, March 1976; (2) Angola, November 1975-February 1976; (3) Nigeria, July 29, 1975; (4) Chad, April 13, 1975; (5) Niger, April 1974; (6) Upper Volta, February 1974; (7) Ethiopia, September 1974; (8) Rwanda, July 1973; (9) Swaziland, April 1973; and (10) Malagasy Republic, June 1975. Save for the bitter civil war in Angola, no change in policy is apparent in the U.S. reaction or lack of reaction to these coups. In fact the U.S. policy of deemphasizing recognition of a new regime has been so successful that when a coup occurs, the question is rarely raised by the press or by other nations. If raised, it is handled in a perfunctory manner.[25]

---

[22] U.S. Department of State, *Telegram from Washington to Accra*, January 27, 1972.

[23] Department of State, *Telegram from Accra to Washington*, January 29, 1972.

[24] Ibid.

[25] In the two most important coups since 1972, Nigeria in 1975 and Ethiopia in 1974, the scenario was followed without alteration. In response to a question from the press on the Ethiopian coup, the State Department spokesman responded: "The United States has enjoyed good relations with the Ethiopian government of Haile Selassie and looks forward to good relations with the new government there . . ." (U.S. Department of State, *For the Press*, September 1974). The spokesman also noted during the press briefing that "at the moment" the

The grant of independence to Angola on November 11, 1975, raised starkly different problems than the United States faced in the "usual" African military coup, and these factors altered U.S. recognition policy. Both before and after Angola achieved independence three major factions vied for control of the state, with each in control of certain identifiable segments of the country. However, upon the grant of independence, the Popular Movement for the Liberation of Angola, backed by the Soviet Union and Cuba and in control of the capital, declared itself the government of Angola. This government was promptly recognized by the Soviet Union and its Eastern European allies.[26]

Almost simultaneously, a coalition of two other nationalist groups, the National Front for the Liberation of Angola (FNLA) and the National Union for the Total Independence of Angola (UNITA) announced the formation of a second government based in southern Angola. This coalition was supported by South Africa, Zaire, and Zambia, and, to a lesser extent, by the United States.

On November 12, U.S. officials announced that the United States would withhold recognition until a government capable of administering the entire country was formed. In taking this position, the United States followed the lead of the Organization of African Unity which suggested that no factional government be accorded recognition. The U.S. officials did announce that if the Popular Movement was ultimately successful in gaining control of the entire country, the United States would accord recognition.[27]

In a news conference later in Pittsburgh, however, Secretary Kissinger suggested another basis for withholding U.S. recognition— the Soviet and Cuban involvement in the civil warfare. Kissinger stated that the United States had decided not to recognize the Angolan faction in control of the capital because the Marxist movement had secured its gains through massive assistance from the Soviet Union and Cuba.[28]

The initial U.S. response by lower State Department officials was in line with established recognition policy, deviating only in that recognition was explicitly mentioned. The reference to recognition was no

---

question of recognition did not arise. The embassy was instructed to continue working-level contacts with the new government. In the Nigerian coup that deposed General Yakubu Gowon, State Department officials indicated that the coup would not result in any basic change in U.S.-Nigerian relations (*Washington Post*, July 30, 1975).

[26] *Washington Post*, November 12, 1975, p. A1.

[27] Ibid.

[28] Ibid., November 13, 1975, p. A2.

doubt a result of the world attention focused on the civil war, and the U.S. relationship to the warring factions. In other ways, the initial announcement, that the United States would recognize whatever regime was in effective control of the entire country, was in accord with established policy of not using recognition as a policy tool.

Secretary Kissinger's criterion, not to recognize a new government because it seized power with the help of outside forces, represents a throwback to earlier policy, especially that of the Truman administration which refused recognition to new governments because of outside involvement.

The issue of recognition of a new government in Angola was a bitter and divisive one for Africans. By the end of November, Nigeria, Mozambique, Guinea-Bissau, Guinea, and Mali had recognized the Popular Movement for the Liberation of Angola (MPLA). No state had recognized the rival National Union for the Total Independence of Angola (UNITA) or the National Front for the Liberation of Angola (FNLA).[29] By January, as the MPLA was gaining the military advantage, twenty-one of the then forty-six African states had recognized the MPLA.[30]

On February 12, Secretary of State Kissinger reiterated his stand that the United States would not recognize the MPLA because of the 12,000 Cuban troops in Angola and the $300 million worth of Soviet equipment there. He did indicate that when a true de facto situation presented itself the United States would reconsider its policy. In essence, the U.S. objection and the refusal to recognize was based not on the "African component of the government" but "the outside imposition of a government."[31]

---

[29] Ibid., November 27, 1975, p. A15.

[30] Ibid., January 9, 1976, p. A1.

[31] U.S. Department of State, *Press Conference*, February 12, 1976. The full exchange as reported:

Q. "In light of the diplomatic and military successes of the Popular Movement [for the Liberation of Angola—MPLA] in Angola, is the United States prepared to follow the OAU [Organization of African Unity] line and recognize the MPLA as the legitimate government of Angola, or at least open diplomatic contacts with them?"

A. "The United States has declared consistently that its objection was not to the MPLA as an organization, nor to its political views as such. Our objection has been to the imposition of a minority government by what is now 12,000 Cuban troops and nearly $300 million worth of Soviet equipment. Since January alone the Soviet Union has introduced over $100 million worth of military equipment into Angola.

"Those facts will not be changed by the military victory that will inevitably result when one side is deprived of restraint and the other is given no opportunity to resist.

"What the United States will do when a [de facto] situation exists, we will

122

The United States did not limit its efforts to influence the Angolan situation to its refusal to extend recognition. The State Department also attempted to persuade Common Market states to withhold recognition. The attempt failed. Reportedly, the secretary urged Common Market countries to maintain a common position on the issue of recognition. However, this approach was rejected on the theory that the best way of removing Soviet and Cuban influence was to free the MPLA from dependence on the Russians and Cubans. The best way to accomplish this, many believed, would be to accept the new government, establish diplomatic relations, and develop trade ties.[32]

In many ways, the United States refusal to recognize the MPLA illustrates the more general failings of recognition to achieve policy ends. In the Angolan situation the continuing U.S. refusal to recognize cut off most contact with the new government and prevented the establishment of diplomatic and trade ties, as well as possible aid agreements. The policy isolated the United States and placed it in opposition to the position taken by most other states. Arguably, it hardened the hostility of the MPLA toward the United States and ensured that the regime would continue to depend on Communist support, assuming Western European ties were not sufficient, as expected. The crudity and blunderbuss effect of nonrecognition is readily apparent in the Angolan situation as it has been on most occasions when it has been invoked.

Other Parts of the World

The United States pursued a similar policy of refusal to recognize a government in effective control after the April 1975 collapse of the Thieu government in South Vietnam, and the collapse and overthrow of the Lon Nol government and its temporary successor in Cambodia. Following the collapse of the Thieu government, the U.S. Treasury froze all South Vietnamese assets in this country and Secretary Kissinger announced that the United States would hold off on any decision to extend recognition to the new rulers in Saigon.[33] Somewhat earlier, at a meeting of European ministers in Dublin, the United

---

decide under those circumstances. But I have said before our objection is to the outside imposition of a government and not to the African component of the government itself."

[32] *Washington Post*, February 26, 1976.

[33] Ibid., May 8, 1975, p. A2.

States had asked the nine European Common Market countries to withhold recognition of the Viet Cong government.[34]

Following the victory of the Communists in South Vietnam, Great Britain and France accorded quick recognition to the new Saigon government,[35] as did Australia, which acted even before the final collapse of the Thieu government.

There were conflicting indications from the Department of State on recognition or normalization of relations with the governments in South Vietnam and Cambodia. In March 1976 Secretary Kissinger announced that the United States was prepared "in principle" to normalize relations with North Vietnam. In contrast, in April 1976 President Ford denied that the United States was preparing to recognize or normalize relations with Hanoi.[36] The "recognition" of the new Cambodian government received less attention; however, the United States has continued to refuse to extend recognition because of political factors.

Events overtook the United States decision-making process on the recognition of the new government of South Vietnam, however. The two parts of Vietnam were unified, and the question of recognition of the new government of South Vietnam was mooted. The issue that remained was the normalization of relations with the state of Vietnam.

In other, less significant changes of government in parts of the world other than Africa and Latin America, the United States appears to have adhered to its policy of deemphasizing recognition. Since early 1969, coups have occurred in Pakistan, March 1969; Afghanistan, July 1974; Bangladesh, August 1975; Bangladesh, November 1975; Portugal, April 1974; and Lebanon, March 1976. In none of the coups did the United States withhold recognition or make a major policy initiative using recognition as a bargaining chip.

Conclusion

Today the U.S. attitude toward military-backed changes of government as reflected in recognition policy seems well established. In cases in which the United States does not perceive major policy interests at stake, it will accept the new regime without strong protest, resume relations, and deemphasize the entire recognition process. In the few instances in which the United States perceives major political

---

[34] Ibid., April 17, 1975, p. A6.
[35] Ibid., May 14, 1975, p. A1.
[36] Ibid., April 25, 1976, p. A11.

interests at issue, the United States has shown a tendency to revive the use of recognition to pursue policy goals.

In the great majority of extraconstitutional changes of government, the U.S. policy of deemphasizing recognition and continuing relations has worked well. While at times the approach has suffered from conceptual ambiguity and semantic confusion, today the United States is able to resume relations with the new government quickly and without making an affirmative decision to recognize, thereby avoiding the political problems that have characterized those decisions. Thus the United States maintains contact with the new government and gradually expands the channels through which the new government can be reached until relations are fully normalized.

5

RECOGNITION PRACTICE OF OTHER STATES

General Comments

This study concerns itself mainly with the recognition practice of the United States. However, it is useful to examine the recognition policy and practices of other states to provide a framework in which to analyze U.S. policy. In suggesting changes in U.S. policy, it is appropriate to examine the approaches adopted by other states and to assess their effectiveness.

The various approaches detailed in Appendix A are based on two sources: a 1969 circular telegram sent to all U.S. embassies requesting them to ask the respective foreign ministries about the recognition policy of the state, and a 1975 request by the author to each state's Washington embassy to set out the recognition policy of the state. The latter had the same format as the 1969 telegram.

The following questions were asked:

- Does your country follow the Estrada Doctrine on recognition of foreign governments?
- Is effective control of the state by a new regime a criterion in the grant of recognition by your country?
- Is a willingness to honor international obligations a criterion in the grant of recognition by your country?
- Is the consent of the people of the state in which the extra-constitutional change occurred a criterion in the grant of recognition by your country?
- Does your country distinguish between the recognition of a new government and the establishment of diplomatic relations with that government?

- Does your country consider political factors in the decision to recognize a new government?
- Does your country consider other factors in the decision to recognize a new government? If so, what factors?

The recognition policy of the various nations is best examined through regional groupings. Recognition by all except a few major powers tends to be a regional phenomenon, because small states tend to concern themselves with recognition only near their own territory. Recognition has, generally speaking, been a political judgment based on national interest; small countries, such as Ecuador, have little interest in a change of government in Burundi or Malaysia, where they probably do not have diplomatic representation.

Most states have adopted a flexible, pragmatic approach based almost entirely on national interest considerations. Within this broad framework, practice differs dramatically, because states often define their national interests in conflicting ways. For example, in developing countries the practice varies from the Estrada Doctrine (in which recognition is unrelated to whether the assumption of power or change of government occurred outside the constitution) to, until recently, the Tobar Doctrine (in which recognition is refused to any government that comes to power through extraconstitutional means).

With few exceptions, it is difficult strictly to categorize the practice of states. Most states, even those which claim publicly to follow one particular doctrine or another, deviate from that doctrine in circumstances where the state perceives a political interest. Many states do not formally adhere to any one doctrine or approach.

Of the over one hundred states surveyed in the study, over thirty follow the Estrada Doctrine or something very similar to it. For example, a number of states indicate that they recognize states and not governments. This was considered to be within the category of the Estrada Doctrine. However, a number of the states which follow the same basic approach were not aware that the Estrada Doctrine existed. The thirty states that follow the Estrada Doctrine do not seem to be grouped in any one region, nor do they appear to be divided along developed or developing state lines. Most states which follow the Estrada Doctrine are developing; however, this may simply reflect the numerical superiority of developing states. Among developed countries, France, the Federal Republic of Germany, Poland, and Finland follow the Estrada Doctrine to a significant degree in their recognition practice. States in Africa that follow some variation of the Estrada Doctrine include Burundi, Cameroon, Central African Republic (Empire), the Congo, Dahomey, Ethiopia, and others. In Latin

America, Guatemala, Honduras, Mexico, and Peru follow the Estrada Doctrine. In the Far East, Laos follows it.

Categorizing states as adherents of the Estrada Doctrine does not mean that the states do not depart from the doctrine when they consider it in their self interest. In the past, for example, the Federal Republic of Germany, Guatemala, and Ethiopia have explicitly recognized governments when they considered it in their national interest to do so. A number of states also take the position that if a new regime is particularly abhorrent they will depart from the Estrada Doctrine and make a judgment based upon this criterion. Nigeria typifies this approach.

The second major recognition category comprises states that attempt to avoid the recognition question and deemphasize the importance of recognition. Over twenty states fall within this category. The actual technique used to downplay the importance of recognition varies in proportion to the creativity and imagination of the respective foreign offices.

The United States has moved in this direction in recent years. This approach often involves an initial statement that the state is studying the situation in the country where the coup took place. After a period of time, varying from a week to a month generally, the recognizing state then announces that "relations are normal," "relations are continuing," "we are resuming relations," or "the question of recognition did not arise." A number of states indicate there is no significant difference between granting recognition and continuing relations. Other states that attempt to downplay the importance of recognition do make a distinction but blur it in practice. The practice of downplaying recognition fades into the Estrada Doctrine in effect though not in principle. Over fifty states, more than half the states considered in this study, follow a policy of downplaying recognition or disregarding the recognition question entirely.

As for the remaining states, most fall within the general category of traditional recognition policy. Many states that explicitly set the traditional recognition policy criteria out as their public position in reality downplay the recognition question and in effect are close to the Estrada Doctrine. Others that espouse the traditional policy make a good faith inquiry to see if the various criteria are met. If they are, a political judgment is made whether to grant recognition. In different situations, states may emphasize one criterion over another, blurring the legal and political factors. Thus, the specific legal criteria—effective control and honoring international obligations—may be met, but a country may still refuse recognition on political grounds. Other states, such as Canada, adhere more to the legal criteria and make political judgments only in rare cases. However, most observers believe that nations in this group emphasize the political judgment at the expense of the legal. This survey supports that conclusion.

The political considerations involved in a recognition decision vary substantially. For example, the recognition policy of the Republic of China (Taiwan) is governed almost entirely by its desire to have other governments recognize it. Consequently, Taiwan will recognize almost any country that is willing to recognize it and not the People's Republic of China. The same basic consideration applies to South Korea in its competition with North Korea for recognition. Thus it is fair to say that for a small number of states special factors will govern recognition. In the majority of cases, however, political considerations vary, depending on such factors as the recognizing country's relationship with the country in which the coup occurred, the political leanings of the regimes' leaders, the economic relationship between the two countries, and the recognition action taken by other states in the region, as well as by the superpowers, especially the United States.

No country today follows the Tobar or Betancourt Doctrine. Venezuela and Costa Rica, until the mid 1960s, followed the doctrine, which, as mentioned before, uses the principles of legitimacy and intervention to protect constitutional rule and democratic processes.

However, this is not to say that legitimacy is without effect in the recognition of foreign government. States that adhere to the traditional recognition policy may use the criteria of consent of the people as a tool to achieve varying degrees of legitimacy. For example, the United States in the early 1960s in a substantial number of cases insisted upon free elections or a promise of free elections as a condition to the grant of recognition. The U.S. response to the coup in Peru in 1962 exemplifies this approach. However, the general trend seems to be away from legitimacy and intervention and toward the deemphasis or elimination of recognition.

Latin America

Recognition practice in Latin America is governed by a number of factors either unique to Latin America itself or shared with other developing countries. The existence of the United States has a significant influence on the recognition practice of Latin American states. Other states in Latin America look very closely and very quickly to what the U.S. position is on the recognition of a new regime. In many cases, the states specifically request the United States to coordinate its decision with that of other Latin American states. In some cases, anti-

American sentiment is so strong that even though the United States and the Latin American states involved have reached the same policy conclusion, the Latin American states want to make the announcement in advance in order to avoid the impression of being under the thumb of the United States.

The influence of the United States on the recognition practice of Latin America is negative in the sense that many of the recognition practices now utilized in Latin America result from earlier abuses that the United States permitted in its recognition policy. The Estrada Doctrine is the best example of negative reaction to U.S. recognition policy.

In addition to the influence that the United States exerts, Resolution XXVI of the Organization of American States affects the recognition practice of Latin American states. The resolution states in pertinent part:

Article II

1. To recommend to the member states, that, immediately after the overthrow of a government and its replacement by *de facto* government, they begin an exchange of views on the situation, giving due consideration to whether or not the overthrow of the government took place with the complicity and aid of one or more foreign governments, or of their respective officers or agents. To recommend that the governments of the member states, in the exchange of views provided for in the preceding article, considering the following circumstances:

a. whether the *de facto* government proposes to take the necessary measures for the holding of elections within a reasonable period, giving its people the opportunity freely to participate in the consequent electoral process; and

b. whether the *de facto* government agrees to fulfill the international obligations assumed previously by the country, to respect the human rights expressed in the American Declaration of the rights and duties of man, and to comply with the commitments assumed by the signatories of the Declaration to the people of the Americas and the general principles of the Charter of Punta del Este.

3. To recommend that, once opinions have been exchanged, each government decides whether it will maintain diplomatic relations with the *de facto* government.

The resolution is a somewhat surprising document. Section 1(a) of Article II sets out as an appropriate consideration whether the new regime proposes to hold elections within a reasonable period of time, giving the people a chance to participate in the electoral processes freely. Under the traditional approach to recognition, this criterion would fit within the standard of consent of the people. While this criterion has had an ambiguous history, and was meant to reflect only the effectiveness of the new government, it has been used to support legitimacy. Consequently, one might anticipate considerable Latin American hostility to it.

Article II, paragraph 1(b) provides that the de facto government must agree to fulfill the international obligations assumed previously by the state. The principle has its origin in U.S. practice, which sought to ensure that the economic interests of the United States would not be threatened or hindered by the new regime. This was bitterly resented in Latin America in the late 1890s and early 1900s, and the aftereffects linger today.

Taken together these two articles represent separate aspects of traditional recognition policy that had their origins in U.S. practice and that have been, at various times, actively opposed in Latin America.

Resolution XXVI has had little impact on the substantive factors considered in the decision to recognize. The consultations mentioned in the resolution have in practice been almost entirely bilateral. In some cases, the consultation has been prefunctory; in other instances states have made a good faith attempt to communicate their views. However, much consultation of this sort took place even before the resolution was passed.

Some states, including Chile, Colombia, Dominican Republic, El Salvador, and Nicaragua indicate that they follow the substantive criteria of recognition, that is, effective control, acquiescence of the people, and willingness to honor international obligations. This, however, merely reflects traditional recognition practices. Thirteen states indicate that they follow this traditional practice or base their decisions on Resolution XXVI which embodies the traditional criteria.

Only three countries explicitly follow the Estrada Doctrine: Peru, Mexico, and Trinidad and Tobago. Honduras indicates that it follows the doctrine in policy. This lack of adherence to the doctrine is surprising since the Estrada Doctrine originated in Latin America and in Latin American hostility to the intervention of the United States in their domestic affairs.

One might suggest that the reason the countries have been unwilling to accept the Estrada Doctrine is the hesitance of each state to relinquish recognition as a political weapon. Although the use of recognition for political purposes has produced few positive results, and in many cases has been counterproductive, the myth remains that recognition is a potent political tool that can advance the foreign policy interests of a state. Even though the United States has moved toward minimizing the significance of recognition, it has not totally abandoned the political use of recognition. Many Latin American states seem to have taken the same course.

A number of states, such as Argentina, Brazil, and Costa Rica, consider the new regime's respect for human rights as a criterion. This also was specifically mentioned in Resolution XXVI. The consideration of human rights is, to some extent, a judgment on the internal affairs of the state in which the coup occurred. In other words, it represents a shift from the position that a change of government is an internal affair to the proposition that other states have some interest in the change of government. This apparent inconsistency between traditional Latin American insistence on nonintervention and the emphasis placed on respect for human rights by Latin American countries, both unilaterally and through Resolution XXVI, illustrates conflicting policies which most states have not yet reconciled.

Another important consideration in recognition practice is the action of the other states in the region. In the great majority of cases, if a state within a region does not perceive a primary political interest, its position will merely be to wait until a number of states have recognized the new government or announced that they are resuming relations or continuing relations. Then it will attempt to act somewhere in the middle of the group, and it will, in almost all cases, attempt to avoid being among the last to recognize, since it does not wish to harm relations with the new regime. Of course, if the nation perceives a primary political interest, the political factor will usually override legal criteria. Thus, a state will often grant quick recognition to a regime it favors if there are no tricky political crosscurrents or major political disadvantages involved.

Respect for international obligations or the willingness to fulfill international obligations is cited as a criterion far more often by Latin American countries than by countries in other regions, probably because of U.S. influence. Its acceptance evidently reflects a Latin American belief in the value of international law. It also provides a degree of stability in the conduct of relations between states.

Africa

Thirty-four states were examined in Africa. Of these thirty-four, nineteen stated that they had adopted the Estrada Doctrine. This contrasts with Latin America, where only three states explicitly follow the Estrada Doctrine. A number of the nineteen African states adhering to the principle were unaware of the existence of the Estrada Doctrine itself. Other states appeared to be unclear about the doctrine. For example, in response to the question whether it followed the Estrada Doctrine, a state might answer yes, but then list specific criteria when asked what criteria it used to grant recognition. The criteria could be those used for maintaining diplomatic relations. Other states, such as the Malagasy Republic, stated that although they followed the Estrada Doctrine, they would depart from it under given political circumstances. Others, such as Kenya, attempted to avoid the question of recognition whenever possible. Again, as in Latin America, there is a continuum, varying from a strict application of the Estrada Doctrine to the more interventionary side of traditional recognition policy.

A striking difference between African and Latin American recognition policy is the lack of emphasis on willingness to fulfill international obligations. Only six of the thirty-three African states indicated that this was a criterion to any extent at all.

Fourteen African states which have not formally accepted the Estrada Doctrine adhere to the basic principle of the doctrine. A number of these states, such as Ghana, Kenya, Libya, and Senegal, attempt to avoid the recognition question whenever possible.

States such as Zambia, which follow an ad hoc policy based on their national interest, indicated that they emphasize moral and political considerations in deciding to grant recognition. In certain instances, a state that normally follows the Estrada Doctrine may be so politically or morally outraged by the circumstances of a change of government that it will express its dislike for a particular regime by refusing recognition.

There are a few African states that have developed a sophisticated doctrine. For example, Rwanda accepts the Estrada Doctrine. In its explanation of its recognition policy, Rwanda indicates that it bases its decision on resuming diplomatic relations at first on effective control and then upon other policy matters. Rwanda explicitly rejects political considerations in recognition. Gabon is the only state that indicates it consistently follows the Estrada Doctrine, regardless of political consideration. The other states that follow the Estrada Doctrine, such as Ethiopia, Malagasy Republic, Kenya, Ivory Coast, and a number of others, will deviate from Estrada for political reasons.

Why is the Estrada Doctrine more popular in Africa than in Latin America? One might hazard a guess that since coups are even more frequent in Africa than in Latin America, it is helpful to have a doctrine that can be applied to the majority of coups, give continuity, and minimize friction. Lending support to this theory is the statement by the leaders of Togo and Niger that they have adopted the Estrada Doctrine because of the numerous coups in Africa.

On the other hand, many states feel it is necessary to retain a degree of discretion in which recognition can be used as a tool to express political values. Although the majority of states in Africa have accepted the Estrada Doctrine, some have explicitly retained the right to deviate from it when they consider it in their best political interest to do so.

Europe

Europe occupies a somewhat anomalous position in recognition practice. Recognition in large part is a regional phenomenon. That is, recognition of a new regime in any given instance will, as a practical matter, be of importance only to the neighboring states and to a lesser extent other areas or countries in that particular region. Europe, of course, is a developed, industrialized civilization in which coups were rare if not nonexistent in the last decade. There were, for example, the 1968 takeover of Czechoslovakia, the change of government in Bulgaria in 1962, the 1967 coup in Greece, and the 1974 coup in Portugal. However, most states did not consider the question of recognition to arise in these instances, and thus Europe does not have much recent experience with the question of recognition within its own region.

Several European countries, however, have global interests, and as a result are concerned with changes of government in other regions of the world. Great Britain and the Federal Republic of Germany are examples of this, as is France, especially in Africa. European powers tend to be involved in areas in which they hold colonial interests. Generally, the major states, such as France, Great Britain, and the Federal Republic of Germany, will make recognition decisions on changes of government in Latin America and Africa.

Of the twenty-four states considered to be European in this classification, only four stated that they explicitly followed the Estrada Doctrine. Two of the four, the Federal Republic of Germany and Belgium, indicated that they make exceptions in applying the doctrine on occasion. In Belgium, diplomatic relations are determined on a basis of effective control and popular assent of the people, with national interest an additional factor. The Federal Republic of Germany has adopted the same doctrine, but before diplomatic relations are established two questions must be answered: Is the government in power, and is it in the best interest of the Federal Republic of Germany to have diplomatic relations? France follows the Estrada Doctrine although some officials veer away from explicitly stating this; instead they merely say that France recognizes states and not governments. France's adoption of this approach has met with success in Africa, where it had a considerable colonial interest. Ireland and Portugal have similar policies in that they recognize states and not governments, but officials do not regard this as following the Estrada Doctrine. Italy uses the Estrada Doctrine in various cases, but does not consider it controlling. Political factors often override legal considerations in the decision to grant recognition. The majority of European nations indicate that they follow a traditional or ad hoc policy based on pragmatic considerations of national interest.

Great Britain follows the traditional approach, with the emphasis on effective control. Great Britain has tended to play down recognition as has the United States, although Great Britain does believe an overt act of recognition is needed. However, officials have interpreted this statement to mean a mere acknowledgment of a note, which usually continues diplomatic relations. No formal note is usually sent. Thus, British practice, to a large degree, parallels the practice of the United States.

The Communist countries do not differ substantially from the traditional practice. Bulgaria has a flexible approach and often attempts to play down the issue. Political considerations are the most important factor in the decision and the action of the Soviet Union is especially important in determining Bulgarian reaction. Czechoslovakia follows basically the same pattern. Poland has a somewhat different slant, at least in theory, in that it indicates it will not apply political considerations; if a government is in effective control it will recognize. Polish authorities specifically noted that this differed from the American practice of considering political practices. The Soviet Union has a pragmatic approach, in which self-interest is the guiding factor. Yugoslavia also follows this approach.

Near East and South Asia

Of the eighteen countries classified in the Near East and South Asia region, only three follow the Estrada Doctrine. Two of these, Kuwait and Nepal, indicate that they make exceptions based on political considerations or national interest. Nepal has not formally adopted the Estrada Doctrine but tends to follow the basic principles. Turkey seems to have adopted the most doctrinally pure approach and has stated that the question of recognition criteria does not arise under the Estrada Doctrine, since only diplomatic relations are considered. On the other hand, Kuwait makes exceptions for political reasons. The other nations follow the same pattern seen in Africa, Latin America, and Europe, an ad hoc policy based on political considerations. Israel exemplifies this practice. In the Near East the reaction of other Arab states to changes in Arab governments is especially important, perhaps even more so than regional reactions in Latin America and Africa.

Far East

Of the thirteen countries in the Far East classification, only two stated that they would follow, or do follow, the Estrada Doctrine—Indonesia and Laos. Both indicated, however, that they do not strictly adhere to the doctrine and would in certain instances consider political factors and make a recognition decision. Australia is very close to the Estrada Doctrine, since it looks only to the question whether the government was in power and would stay in power. The Australian government determined that if the government met these two requirements, it would grant recognition without considering political factors. In fact one might look on the Australian position as closer to absolute noninterference with the internal affairs of another state than the position taken by states that accept the Estrada Doctrine but make exceptions in given circumstances. Japan, which until 1965 made an explicit recognition decision in each case, has since that date deemphasized recognition and no longer explicitly sends a note granting recognition. Japan does not have fixed criteria or a formal doctrine, and like other countries makes an ad hoc political decision. In doing so, Japan looks to the actions of the neighboring states and of the United States. The other states in the Far East utilize no set criteria, and make the recognition decision basically on political grounds. The Philippines is a good example of this, as are Thailand, Malaysia, and South Korea.

Conclusion

The practice of states in the recognition of foreign governments resists categorization. However, certain general tendencies are evident. First, few states rigidly adhere to the Estrada Doctrine. Most states that express allegiance to the doctrine consider political factors and grant recognition in certain situations. Other states that do not adhere to the Estrada Doctrine deemphasize the recognition to such an extent that they in effect have moved very close to the principle of the doctrine. However, it is fair to say that the bulk of the countries follow an ad hoc process in which no specific criteria are given and in which political considerations override legal criteria. No state today follows the Tobar or Betancourt Doctrine. While various states will on occasion, because of political factors, emphasize a legitimist or constitutional criterion, this practice is on the decline. In each region the movement is toward deemphasizing or completely eliminating the recognition issue. However, it is doubtful that the recognition question will be eliminated in the forseeable future because, in a significant minority of cases, nations consider the political factors strong enough to make an issue of recognition. This desire to deemphasize recognition in the majority of cases has resulted in the adherence of over thirty states to the Estrada Doctrine, but with the proviso that in certain situations they grant recognition based on political considerations. The desire to deemphasize recognition also affects the adherence of well over thirty other states to an ad hoc policy based on political considerations in which recognition is usually downplayed and finessed by the euphemism that relations are continuing, or that relations are being resumed. Taken together, the two approaches account for over seventy-five of the states included in this study.

Appendix A to this volume provides a survey of the recognition policy of over one hundred states for 1969 and 1975. The table shows whether the country adheres to the Estrada Doctrine and gives the traditional criteria for recognition policy. Also included are questions whether the state makes a distinction between diplomatic relations and recognition, whether the nation considers a political factor in its formula for granting recognition, and other information that the state considers important for its recognition decision.

States that seemingly follow the traditional recognition policy may actually rely on only one or two of the criteria in making recognition decisions. Some states follow the Estrada Doctrine but also list criteria for the recognition of governments. This may simply reflect the criteria for continuing diplomatic relations, but it is doubtful if it is clear even in the minds of the officials administering the policy.

The appendix reflects other inconsistencies in a number of practices. This results not from an inadequacy in the gathering of data, but rather from a basic truth about the recognition practice of various states: it is largely an ad hoc procedure, governed by political considerations.

6
U.S. RECOGNITION POLICY FOR THE FUTURE

President Kennedy, departing from the practice of Eisenhower and Truman, among others, utilized recognition to promote constitutional government, especially in Latin America. Succeeding presidents rejected this approach, gradually moving toward a policy of deemphasizing recognition and resuming relations with whichever regime was in effective control. Where policy makers perceived significant national interest in a change of government, nonrecognition was resurrected as a policy tool. In the great majority of instances, however, the United States has followed a recognition policy that, in the words of one State Department official, is "largely indistinguishable" from the Estrada Doctrine. In short, the recognition of foreign governments that come to power through extraconstitutional means no longer plays a meaningful role in American foreign policy.

In rejecting the use of recognition to further policy ends, the United States has never officially adopted the Estrada Doctrine, although it has stated publicly that when an extraconstitutional change of government occurs, the United States concerns itself more with the continuance of relations than with recognizing the new government. This chapter will consider two basic questions: Should this policy be continued into the 1980s? and, Are there any changes that should be made in the policy?

Even a summary glance at the U.S. response to extraconstitutional changes of government in the past decade reveals that it has been strikingly successful in downplaying the recognition issue and resuming diplomatic relations with a minimum of disruption or publicity. As the United States gradually deemphasized recognition and stressed the continuity of relations with the new regime, interest in the U.S. action among other states and the press waned. The presumption came to be that the change of government would be treated matter-of-factly, and that relations would be continued with as little fuss as possible. With this expectation now firmly ingrained in the minds of other states and the press, the U.S. policy of deemphasizing recognition and resuming relations quietly can be considered effective.

The question must be asked, however, whether the United States has relinquished anything of value in declining to use recognition as a political instrument in responding to changes in government. Secondly, should the United States continue to use recognition as a weapon in instances where it perceives major values at stake?

Recognition is not now, nor is it likely to become, an effective instrument by which to advance American foreign policy interests. One State Department official said the incentive for U.S. recognition has proved singularly ineffective

> in influencing new governments; at best it elicits vague promises of support and friendship. Whatever the force of the argument may have been in the early 1900s particularly in the Western Hemisphere, the prospect of recognition by the United States is no longer an effective leverage through which to influence a new regime.[1]

In the past, the requirement to make a decision on recognition of a new government often placed the United States in an awkward position, forcing it to act within a limited span of time and within certain set substantive standards. Typically, before the United States adopted its policy of downplaying recognition, a new regime often centered its attention, as did other states, on whether the United States had decided to recognize the regime. In making this decision, the U.S. range of action was considerably restricted. The United States could not afford to be isolated, and thus had to orchestrate its response with the actions of other states, often within a matter of a few weeks, and usually before it had a clear idea of what policies the new government would pursue. In particular instances, the United States had to make its response in a climate of emotion generated by a return to rightist military government, by a brutal overthrow, or by any number of other circumstances. Eliminating recognition as a policy instrument had the desirable consequence of allowing the United States to deal with a new government on a variety of levels over a longer period of time, gradually establishing a relationship that more accurately reflects true policy interests.

Second, utilizing recognition as a political tool raises the specter of nonrecognition. Should the United States withhold recognition

---

[1] U.S. Department of State, Office of the Legal Adviser, Memorandum, June 1, 1971.

permanently where a new government refuses to make certain concessions? Or should the United States refuse recognition where the new government achieved power through brutal means or is otherwise morally abhorrent? Is nonrecognition an effective means of removing such a regime from power, and if so is this a legitimate goal of U.S. foreign policy?

Nonrecognition is a drastic sanction, and in practice normally cuts off contact between the two states involved. Most agree that nonrecognition has been ineffective in the instances in which it has been used. According to Senator Cranston,

> The evidence is overwhelming that withholding recognition from governments of which we disapprove, and with whom our relations are particularly hostile, has failed totally to advance our values or to achieve any other significant and enduring purposes.
>
> Indeed, nonrecognition makes it difficult for us to transmit our values and to state clearly our purposes. It deprives us of an opportunity to determine accurately the effectiveness of our actions. It prevents us not only from exerting influence but from gaining insight.[2]

As one State Department official noted,

> the threat of nonrecognition is even less effective [than concessions gained from the grant of recognition] and may precipitate hostile statements or responses. Nonrecognition also results in forsaking the opportunity that diplomatic relations offer for influencing the attitudes and conduct of the new regime. In addition this action may well exacerbate the very tendency of the regime which militated against recognition in the first place. In short, nonrecognition prevents the United States from exerting influence and gaining insights and deprives the United States of an opportunity to determine the effectiveness of our actions.[3]

To those that argue that nonrecognition should be used as a policy response in extreme cases of cruelty or brutality, the statement by Lauterpacht is adequate refutation:

> So long as international law does not stigmatize revolutions as being in the nature of crimes against the law of nations, it cannot condemn the means, necessarily violent, by which revolutions are achieved. Respect for the sanctity of human

---

[2] Senate Committee on Foreign Relations, *Hearings on S. Res. 205*, p. 5.
[3] U.S. Department of State, Office of the Legal Adviser, Memorandum, June 1, 1971.

life is not a natural concomitant of revolutionary upheavals. When the revolutionary regime lends itself to acts of cruelty and savagery which shock the moral sense of the civilized world, mere refusal of recognition is an ineffective and inadequate substitute for immediate supression of the evil by a determined act of intervention. Short of that radical remedy, refusal to recognize is a stimulus to rather than a check upon barbarity. It deprives states adopting that attitude of the opportunity for intercession and for appeal to the sense of humanity and pity of the revolutionary authorities. Finally, unless humanitarian intervention is made a rule of international practice to a larger extent than it is at present, it is difficult to see why drastic disapproval on the part of foreign nations by means of nonrecognition or withdrawal of recognition should be restricted to cases of inhuman conduct in the course of a revolution, and leave untouched barbarous suppression of opponents and minorities by an apparently well-established regime.[4]

There are other reasons for abandoning recognition. Recognition is an old and oft-used concept that has generated much hostility and emotion in the course of its use. As a consequence of changing policies, recognition has come to mean strikingly different things to the states, the press, and the public. Thus, in certain recent instances where the United States merely wished quietly to resume relations it has not wished to recognize the new regime publicly, since in the eyes of some, recognition connotes approval of a new regime, its policies, and the manner in which it achieved power.

One of the major problems historically associated with the use of recognition as a policy instrument has been the charge of intervention in the domestic affairs of other states. Some Latin American diplomats and scholars have charged that the act of recognition itself constitutes intervention. Of course, the extent of intervention in a given instance will vary substantially, depending on the substantive goals that the recognizing state is attempting to advance.

U.S. manipulation of two of the normal criteria for granting recognition has resulted in numerous acts of intervention. Acquiescence of the people in the change of government has been interpreted by the United States on occasion, especially during the Kennedy presidency, to mean that a new regime will not be recognized unless the people ratify the change of government through elections. In pursuit of this aim, the United States has used recognition as a bargaining chip to obtain promises for election from the new regime.

---

[4] Lauterpacht, *Recognition in International Law*, p. 107.

This typically involves wrangling over the timing of elections, safeguards to assure their fairness, and even disputes over which candidates would run. Certainly, such action constitutes substantial involvement in the electoral process, perhaps the most sovereign act of an independent state.

Reliance on the acquiescence of the people to promote constitutional government and to discourage extraconstitutional changes of government amounts, in essence, to a revival of legitimism, in a different form. In whatever form, however, legitimism has for its major purpose the discouragement of revolution and the maintenance of the existing order of government. For Woodrow Wilson and John Kennedy, the existing order of government to be preserved was constitutional democracy; for the European states of the eighteenth century the existing order to be preserved was monarchy. If the basic premise is accepted that a state under international law has the right to choose its own government free of external interference, it follows that the doctrine of legitimacy infringes a fundamental right of states.

Whether or not passing judgment on the constitutionality of the government of another state constitutes intervention, such a judgment often proves a practical impossibility. As Philip Jessup once noted, determining whether to accord recognition by inquiry into the legitimacy of origin of the new government is "bad international politics and may actually put the recognizing state in the impossible position of attempting to pass on constitutional provisions of another state."[5]

Intervention has been more blatant in the case of the second criterion—willingness to honor international obligation—and here motives of the United States have typically been less pristine. The criterion, adopted by the United States in the late nineteenth century to advance American business and economic interests in Latin America and the Caribbean, has been manipulated by the United States to gain economic advantages for American business interests. As one scholar commented:

> There is only one step between proclaiming the latter [willingness to fulfill international obligations] as a condition of recognition and the insistence on the fulfillment of what is claimed to be a particular obligation to the recognizing state; and there is often only one further step between the latter and the requirement of compliance with an arbitrary political demand unrelated to any true claim of right.[6]

---

[5] Philip C. Jessup, *A Modern Law of Nations* (New York: MacMillan Co., 1948), p. 57.

[6] Lauterpacht, *Recognition in International Law*, p. 161.

The United States has overstepped itself repeatedly. However, in recent years, where the United States has not perceived a significant economic or financial interest in a change of government, a *pro forma* statement issued by the new government has been routinely accepted by the United States. In such cases, the criterion is meaningless.

There are other problems in utilizing the acquiescence of the people and the willingness of the new government to honor international obligations as criteria on which to base a decision to recognize a new government. In some cases the acquiescence criteria may be meaningless. The people may be passive, politically ignorant, or uninformed.

A like problem inheres in the willingness to honor international obligations. The international obligations of the state are binding on the new regime whether or not it announces its intention to fulfill them. It does not lie within the power of the new government to repudiate the obligations of the predecessor government. Even if the government intends to repudiate the obligations it may still make a self-serving announcement that it will honor international obligations. A State Department policy official noted, regarding international obligations, "Practically every new regime includes an undertaking to respect international commitments in its initial pronouncement. This has become largely a self serving declaration without much meaningful content; the actions of a new government will speak louder than its words."[7]

A former legal adviser to the Department of State, John R. Stevenson, in a discussion with the Advisory Panel on International Law, indicated his opposition to this criterion:

> The willingness to comply with obligations should not be included in any basic test for recognition. It is not up to a government whether it is willing to comply with its obligations; international law requires it to comply; and the international community must compel it to comply. There will still remain the question of the fact of the effectiveness of the new government.[8]

On the positive side, perhaps the most important reason for not utilizing recognition as a policy instrument is that this course reflects the legitimate interests of the United States in addressing the new government. In the overwhelming majority of coups, the United States

---

[7] Ibid.

[8] U.S. Department of State, Office of the Legal Adviser, Meeting of Advisory Panel on International Law, October 27, 1967.

for a variety of reasons does not wish to take significant action. In many instances the United States does not have a significant interest in an extraconstitutional change of government. Typically, successful coups d'etat involve developing states in Africa or Latin America in which one military regime replaces another. The interest of the United States here is simply to continue relations as quietly and unobtrusively as possible. In other coups where the United States might have an interest, it has come to realize that any attempt to gain major policy objectives at the expense of the new regime is met by cries of intervention and proves counterproductive. Again, the major U.S. interest in such cases becomes the quiet continuation of normal relations. Downplaying recognition or eliminating the concept altogether serves this overall policy well. Finally, in the relatively few cases in which the United States does wish to advance given policy interests, other methods have proved far more effective than recognition.

If the United States wishes to make an issue of the nature of the new regime, it may do so in a variety of ways, structuring its response in a manner attuned to the objective it wishes to achieve. For example, if the United States wishes to discourage coups by anti-democratic forces, it could suspend military assistance, decrease aid, reduce its diplomatic mission, or call for action in the Organization of American States or the United Nations. High-level officials could state their disapproval, and announce strong opposition to actions of the new government. The United States could communicate privately with the new regime, expressing its views, a practice more often successful than public moral posturing which hardens a regime's position. It seems certain that such a flexible framework for response by the United States would have a better chance of influencing new regimes than recognition policy.

Problems with Current Policy

As reflected in the preceding chapters, the United States has in the past ten years gradually moved away from the use of recognition as a political instrument save in a limited number of isolated instances. On the whole, this approach has worked well. There are problems with this approach, although to date the problems are more conceptual and theoretical than practical and immediate.

The United States has never officially announced that it has decided to eliminate the concept of recognition of governments that come to power through extraconstitutional means or, positively stated, that it has adopted the Estrada Doctrine. Instead, it has chosen to proceed gradually, and largely without public announcement. Clearly there were advantages to such a policy, some of which no doubt remain. However, this approach, no matter how successful in downplaying recognition or how necessary as a matter of bureaucratic politics, has resulted in a conceptual muddle. If one examines the public statements of State Department officials on the U.S. recognition action and policy in recent years, one is immediately struck by the evasiveness of their replies and by their attempts to obfuscate U.S. action. Indeed, one might say that this was central to U.S. recognition policy. In attempting to downplay recognition the press officers were instructed to deemphasize the recognition concept, not to use the term in exchanges with the press, and to emphasize the continuance of relations. Formal press statements reflected the same practice.

This evasiveness manifested itself in various ways. Typically, following a coup, the State Department would initially announce that it was studying the situation. If asked later by members of the press corps about the status of relations, press officers would say that relations were normal, or that relations had continued or resumed.

If reporters pursued the matter, they were met with statements that did not reflect the actual state of relations with the new government at any particular point in time; the press officer was merely attempting in the best way he knew to evade the question without mentioning recognition. The result was to blur and in some cases to distort understanding. Only if pushed hard, with no avenue of retreat, would the press officer announce that recognition of a new government had occurred. And even when this was conceded, the press officer was cautioned not to mention a particular act or point in time when recognition was accorded.

There has been a similar problem with the situations in which the press officer stated that no question of recognition arose. In most such instances, there was at least some semblance of legal continuity; however, the judgment was not a legal one, but one based on policy. The best method of pursuing the policy of downplaying recognition was to announce that the question never arose, which presumably meant that the change of government was constitutional. But no one seriously contends that the change of government in such cases was in strict conformance with the domestic law of the state in which it occurred. Nevertheless, the United States in numerous cases has made such a public announcement, an approach not calculated to advance the rule of law in international affairs. One searches in vain for guidelines or distinctions in the situations where the United States concluded that no question of recognition arose, that relations were normal, were continued, or were resumed. The only common theme is the emphasis on continuity in diplomatic relations and the deemphasis of recognition. Not surprisingly, this vague policy has led to conceptual problems concerning the U.S. response to an extraconstitutional change of government.

When an extraconstitutional change of government occurs, are diplomatic relations officially suspended? If not, isn't recognition totally irrelevant and doesn't the United States in fact follow the Estrada Doctrine? If diplomatic relations are suspended, does not the United States, at least conceptually, make two decisions: to recognize the new government, and then to resume diplomatic relations? If diplomatic relations are suspended, how does the decision to recognize differ from the decision to resume diplomatic relations? Are aid programs affected if there is a suspension of diplomatic relations?

The simple fact about these questions and others is that the United States does not make fine distinctions in its decisions when a government comes to power through extraconstitutional means. Over the past ten years, the United States has attempted as a matter of policy to blur the distinction between recognition and diplomatic relations. The United States has been remarkably successful in this policy, and on numerous occasions has confused the press and the public about the difference. Not surprisingly, in confusing the public, the Department of State has also confused itself. As Philip Jessup once noted, the tendency to identify the grant of recognition and the acknowledgement of diplomatic relations has caused much difficulty. It continues to do so, at least in a conceptual sense.

Arguments for Adoption of Estrada Doctrine

Recognition has effectively been eliminated in practice from American foreign policy; it should be eliminated in theory as well. Recognition is irrelevant to the present American policy of treating extraconstitutional changes of government in the same manner as regular changes of government.

In deemphasizing recognition the United States has never repudiated the concept and indeed has used recognition as a political tool in certain recent changes of government. However, in most cases recognition has been a formality at best. For example, in Libya in 1969 the United States announced that it had "maintained relations with the government of Libya and looked forward to a continuation of traditionally close ties."[9] The U.S. spokesman was authorized to an-

---

[9] *New York Times*, September 7, 1969, cited in Wadlow, "Recent United States Recognition Policy toward Coups d'Etat," unpublished manuscript, p. 3.

nounce if asked that this amounted to recognition. In such cases the maintenance of diplomatic relations amounts to a de facto application of the Estrada Doctrine and a declaration of recognition is unnecessary. In the above example, the United States should have announced that it would maintain relations with the state of Libya and that it no longer was in the business of recognizing foreign governments that come to power through extraconstitutional means. When coups occur, the United States would simply maintain diplomatic relations and deal with whatever group was in effective control of the governmental machinery.

What effect would there be if the United States no longer recognized governments? Even the total elimination of recognition from American practice would have little impact on our dealings with other states. For instance, there is plainly only one government in effective control of the territory that all agree constitutes a state—Albania. The elimination of recognition from American practice would, of course, mean that the question of recognizing the Albanian government would no longer arise. However, the question whether diplomatic relations should be established would remain and would present a political question to be decided in light of the national interest of the United States.

Similarly, the elimination of recognition would not materially affect U.S. relations with Cuba, where the United States recognizes the government of Fidel Castro as the government of Cuba but does not maintain diplomatic relations. Eliminating recognition would not affect the question whether the United States should resume diplomatic relations with Cuba. The only possible effect would be on the access of Cuba to the courts of the United States, a matter not likely to cause a major problem.

Eliminating recognition would not solve the "divided state" problems that surround states such as Korea, or states that may become rigidly divided in the future. But such a change could have the salutary effect of reducing the complexity of dealing with the divided state, since it would eliminate one needless issue from the basic political considerations involved in diplomatic representation.

Criticism of the Elimination of Recognition

The elimination of recognition of foreign governments that come to power through extraconstitutional means is not a new idea. It was suggested almost a half century ago by the Mexican diplomat, Estrada, and in the course of time, a substantial number of states have adopted his concept. Not surprisingly, however, over this period the Estrada Doctrine—or stated more broadly, the elimination of recognition of governments—has attracted considerable criticism, of both a practical and a theoretical nature.

Perhaps the primary argument advanced against its elimination is that recognition gives the United States political leverage over the new regime. To give up the instrument removes an effective foreign policy tool. But as has been discussed, the effectiveness of the instrument is open to question. More thoughtful objections have been raised by scholars and diplomats such as Philip Jessup: "Fundamentally . . . the Estrada Doctrine seems to contemplate the obliteration of the distinction between change of government by peaceful balloting and change of government by revolution or coup d'etat."[10]

The current U.S. policy of resuming relations with whatever regime is in power obliterates this distinction in virtually the same way the Estrada Doctrine does. One of the basic values of American foreign policy is the need to have diplomatic relations and contacts with governments of which we disapprove and with which we disagree. Certainly today we recognize both states and governments of which we strongly disapprove. The carrying on of diplomatic relations, as one State Department official has said, is a practical, necessary, and effective means of communication between states—it does not and should not signify approbation or carry any moral significance.[11]

Others have argued that in time resuming relations would develop into a practical equivalent to recognition. Thus, the continuance of diplomatic relations would be taken as de facto recognition; the breaking of relations, if it occurred, would be the same as withdrawing recognition.

This is unlikely as a theoretical matter, and it has not occurred in the practice of those states that have adopted the doctrine. In the overwhelming number of extraconstitutional changes of government, diplomatic relations are not broken. The severance of diplomatic relations is invoked only in extreme circumstances. It is true that an analogy can be drawn between nonrecognition that occurs only sparingly and severance of relations. However, the Estrada Doctrine reverses the presumption when a change of government occurs. Under traditional policy, a government is expected to announce that it has recognized the new regime or on the other hand refused to recognize

---

[10] Jessup, *A Modern Law of Nations*, pp. 63–66.
[11] U.S. Department of State, Office of the Legal Adviser, Memorandum, June 1, 1971.

—and this leads to problems. This fact guided the United States in its ten-year effort to evade and downplay the question of recognition. Under the Estrada Doctrine there is no need to evade or obfuscate, since no need arises for the government to make an announcement or take any action.

Another criticism of the doctrine is that a coup raises the question of which faction should receive the credentials of U.S. diplomats and accredit them. Lawyers in the State Department have met this criticism by noting that the U.S. government regards its diplomatic representatives as accredited to a state rather than to a government. Thus, under the doctrine, in the event of a coup or revolution, U.S. diplomats, if accredited to the state, would continue in their posts. If relations were continued, as would occur in the overwhelming majority of cases, diplomats would merely continue in their post and no question of accreditation would arise. Any new representatives sent would be accredited to the authority in effective control.

Philip Jessup has also raised the problem of how the Estrada Doctrine works when there are rival claimants to power:

> Granted that the diplomatic relations would remain un-affected by changes of government, with whom could other foreign diplomats deal? Should they continue to carry on business with the local officials who are in the capital, even if the revolutionists are in de facto control of all of the rest of the country? Should they carry on their business with the revolutionary leaders if the latter seized the capital, although the government to which diplomats were originally accredited retains control of the rest of the country, including seaports? Or should they deal with both sets of officials with respect to problems arising in areas in which they respectively exercise de facto control? And will the constitutional government be quite willing that the foreign representatives should deal with revolutionary leaders in certain parts of the country?[12]

The simple answer to these questions is that such situations rarely occur. In very few instances in the fifteen-year period covered by this study were there serious rivals to power even ten days following the initiation of a coup.

When such situations do arise, the United States, while waiting for the situation to clear, would have a legitimate interest in fact gathering, and in the normal course would communicate, typically on an informal basis, with all factions. Of course, one or more factions

---

[12] Jessup, *A Modern Law of Nations*, p. 73.

might be hostile and might not wish to communicate. Also the United States might favor one faction politically, making communication with another faction difficult, if not impossible. This, however, is beyond the reach of the Estrada Doctrine. Under the doctrine, when there are rival claimants, the U.S. diplomats could communicate informally with all factions for the purposes of gathering information. The United States would avoid formal acts where possible until the factional struggle was resolved. Officials could indicate that the United States was in the process of determining who was in effective control, and that in the meantime it was maintaining informal contacts to protect essential United States interests and the lives of American nationals. This indeed was the initial U.S. response to the civil war in Angola.

When a state becomes divided into two rigidly defined sections with each faction in firm control, a question of recognition of a new state could possibly arise. Barring this, however, if a situation did develop in which a country was seriously divided over a prolonged period, the United States should, like other countries under the Estrada Doctrine, maintain informal contacts with the two regimes in the various sections. It should indicate in public announcements that no one regime was in full control of the territory of the state and that the United States was maintaining informal contacts to protect U.S. interests.

Certainly, it is possible to imagine difficult situations caused by rival claimants to power. Suppose a state is split with 40 percent controlled by the preexisting government, and 60 percent controlled by rebel forces, and aid or military sales agreements come due. Should the United States deal with the preexisting government and pay out its obligations, or refrain? Neither traditional recognition policy nor the Estrada Doctrine solves such problems, and, when encountered, they must be answered on a case-by-case basis in conformity with U.S. national interests, and perhaps the canons of international law. To point to such difficulties as weaknesses in the Estrada Doctrine, however, is misleading.

Another objection often advanced is that dealing with rebel groups lends respectability to their cause and encourages future coups or revolutions. Again, this objection assumes the rare instance where rival claimants to power are stalemated; usually no such problem arises. And as a practical matter, fact gathering by lower embassy officials through unofficial contacts is not likely to lend respectability to rebel factions.

A final set of objections centers on the domestic consequences of eliminating American recognition practice. Some have argued that without the concept of recognition the United States would face serious problems over the assets of the coup state held in the United States and U.S. government assets in that state. For example, two or more contending factions, both claiming to be the legitimate and constitutional government, could claim assets of the state that were located in the United States. A question would then arise over which claimant would be entitled to the assets in the absence of a U.S. government position on recognition.

Lawyers in the State Department have responded to this argument by noting that the courts would be the institutional body confronted with the problem, and traditionally the courts have looked to the State Department for guidance on these questions. If the department has indicated that the United States recognizes the foreign government, this is conclusive on the question of entitlement. In other cases, courts have considerable flexibility in making determinations of governmental entitlement.[13]

Few such cases will arise. The instances in which there is a political stalemate in a state for a sustained period and in which it is impossible for a court to determine which is the legitimate government will be rare. In the few cases that do arise the State Department would in most instances determine that the United States is continuing relations with one faction or another. If the department does not wish to designate one faction or another, it could supply the court with factual data regarding the political situation and let the court make its own decision. In any case the court could freeze the assets until the situation became more clear.

In situations of stalemate, the United States often would not recognize one faction over another even if it were pursuing a traditional recognition policy. Thus, similar issues would arise in the courts even if recognition was retained in American practice.

Conclusion

In responding to military coups d'etat the United States should announce that it is continuing diplomatic relations with the new government. It should indicate that as a result of a gradual evolution of State Department policy it has decided to eliminate from the U.S. diplomatic practice the concept of recognition of foreign governments that come to power through extraconstitutional means.

Then, when a change of government occurred in a foreign state, no question of recognition would arise. Nor would diplomatic rela-

---

[13] Cochran, "The Recognition of States and Governments," pp. 42–79.

tions automatically be affected by an arguably extraconstitutional change of government. In the normal case diplomatic relations would continue unaffected by the change, since the United States conducts diplomatic relations with states and not the governments of states.

In situations in which there is uncertainty or confusion over control of the governmental machinery of a state, the United States would study the matter and attempt to gain an accurate picture of the political situation as quickly as possible. In such circumstances, the United States would refrain from formal acts; however, as a technical matter, diplomatic relations would continue with the state in question.

APPENDIXES

Appendix A

SURVEY OF RECOGNITION POLICY OF STATES—1969, 1975[1]

(Notes for this table begin on p. 177)

LATIN AMERICA

State	Year	Does State Follow Estrada Doctrine?	Is Effective Control a Factor in Grant of Recognition?	Is Willingness to Honor International Obligations a Factor in Grant of Recognition?	Is Consent of the People a Factor in Grant of Recognition?	Is Distinction Made between Recognition and Diplomatic Relations?	Are Political Factors Important in Recognition Decision?	Other Information on Recognition
Argentina	1969	No	Yes—most important.	Yes	No	No—see note 2.	Yes, national interest governs.	See note 2.
Barbados	1969	No						
Bolivia	1969	No				Yes		See note 3.
Brazil	1969	No	Yes	Yes	Yes	Avoids drawing distinction.	Yes	See note 4.
	1975	No	Yes	Yes	Yes	Avoids drawing distinction.	Yes	Not official policy position.
Chile	1969	No	Yes	Yes	Yes	No		Based on Resolution XXVI.

Country	Year				No. Effective control is sufficient.			
	1975	No	Yes	Yes	Yes	Yes	No	See note 5.
Colombia	1969	No	Yes	Yes	Yes	No		Generally follows Resolution XXVI.
Costa Rica	1969	No	Yes	Yes	Yes			See note 6.
Dominican Republic	1969	No	Yes	Yes	Yes	No		Goes by criteria in Resolution XXVI.
	1975	No	Yes	Yes	Yes	No		Goes by criteria in Resolution XXVI.
Ecuador	1969	No	Yes	Yes	Yes	No	National interest may override formula.	Formula usually followed.
	1975	No	Yes	Yes	Yes	No	National interest may override formula.	See note 7.
El Salvador	1969	No	Yes	Yes	Yes	No		See note 8.
Guatemala	1969	Yes		Yes	Yes	No		See note 9.
Haiti	1969	No	Yes	Yes	Yes	No		See note 10.

Appendix A (continued)

State	Year	Does State Follow Estrada Doctrine?	Is Effective Control a Factor in Grant of Recognition?	Is Willingness to Honor International Obligations a Factor in Grant of Recognition?	Is Consent of the People a Factor in Grant of Recognition?	Is Distinction Made between Recognition and Diplomatic Relations?	Are Political Factors Important in Recognition Decision?	Other Information on Recognition
Honduras	1969	No, but follows policy.				Yes		No fixed guidelines—ad hoc.
	1975	No	Yes	Yes	Respect for human rights considered.		No	In certain cases, will consider other factors.
Jamaica	1969	No	Yes			Yes		See note 11.
Mexico	1969	Yes				No—recognition not used.		
	1975	Yes, although tacit recognition.	Yes	Yes	Yes		Yes	No
Nicaragua	1969	No	Yes	Yes	Yes	No	Yes	See note 12.
Panama	1969	No	Yes	Yes	Yes	Yes		Traditional policy, nondoctrine position.

	Year					Self interest most important factor.	
Paraguay	1969	No	Yes	Yes	Yes	Yes	Follows traditional policy. Gov't. must not be tainted by communism.
Peru	1969	Yes	Yes, most important.	Yes	Yes	No	Looks to effective control, acceptance by people.
Trinidad Tobago	1969	Yes					
	1975	Yes					
Uruguay	1969	No	Yes	Yes	Yes	Yes	See note 13.
Venezuela	1969	No	Yes	Yes	Yes	Little distinction.	See note 14.
	1975	No	Yes	Yes	Yes	Little distinction.	
AFRICA							
Algeria	1969	No				Yes	See note 15.
Botswana	1969	No				Yes	See note 16.

Appendix A (continued)

State	Year	Does State Follow Estrada Doctrine?	Is Effective Control a Factor in Grant of Recognition?	Is Willingness to Honor International Obligations a Factor in Grant of Recognition?	Is Consent of the People a Factor in Grant of Recognition?	Is Distinction Made between Recognition and Diplomatic Relations?	Are Political Factors Important in Recognition Decision?	Other Information on Recognition
Burundi	1969	Yes, but ministry unfamiliar with doctrine.				No	No	Diplomatic relations based on national interest.
	1975	See note 17.						
Cameroon	1969	Yes, based on French experience.	Accepts whatever government in effective control.			Slight distinction.		See note 18.
Central African Republic (Empire)	1969	Yes	Yes		Yes	No	Yes	See note 19.
Chad	1969	Issue deferred.						Criteria for maintaining diplomatic relations done on pragmatic

Country	Year					Policy / Comments
Congo	1969	Yes		No	Yes	consideration.
Dahomey	1969	Yes	Yes	No	Yes	Criteria are effective control and self-interest. Wait for other states.
Ethiopia	1969	Yes		No	Yes	Ad hoc; will grant recognition if in self-interest.
Gabon	1969	Yes		No	Yes	Consistently follow Estrada Doctrine.
Ghana	1969	No		Yes	Yes	Pragmatic consideration avoid recognition, traditional policy.
Guinea	1969	No		Yes	Yes	Pragmatic. Based on national interest & moral issues.
Ivory Coast	1969	Yes		Yes	Yes	See note 20.
Kenya	1969	Yes, generally.		No	Yes, may outweigh de facto control.	Pragmatic. Often tries to avoid question.

Appendix A (continued)

State	Year	Does State Follow Estrada Doctrine?	Is Effective Control a Factor in Grant of Recognition?	Is Willingness to Honor International Obligations a Factor in Grant of Recognition?	Is Consent of the People a Factor in Grant of Recognition?	Is Distinction Made between Recognition and Diplomatic Relations?	Are Political Factors Important in Recognition Decision?	Other Information on Recognition
Lesotho	1969	No				No		Question not of great importance; minimal contacts with world community.
Liberia	1969	No				Yes		Maintains continuity of diplomatic relations; pragmatic, based on national interest.
Libya	1969	No, not familiar with doctrine.				Has not considered question.		Attempts to avoid question; no specific act unless state system changes.
								Will recognize in some cases,

Country	Date				Notes
Malagasy Republic	1969	Yes		No, usually.	based on policy factors.
Mali	1969	Yes		No	Might deviate from Estrada for policy factors.
Malta	1969	Yes		No	Ad hoc; no written recognition policy.
Morocco	1969	Partially; "leans to."	Yes	Not finely drawn.	Depends on case and what other countries do.
Niger	1969	Yes		No	Wishes to avoid giving approval to coups in Africa.
	1975	Yes		No	The fundamental principle of Niger is to recognize states.
Nigeria	1969	Yes	Yes	Yes	Yes	Estrada consistent with OAU Doctrine.
Rwanda					Effective control rejects po-

Appendix A (continued)

State	Year	Does State Follow Estrada Doctrine?	Is Effective Control a Factor in Grant of Recognition?	Is Willingness to Honor International Obligations a Factor in Grant of Recognition?	Is Consent of the People a Factor in Grant of Recognition?	Is Distinction Made between Recognition and Diplomatic Relations?	Are Political Factors Important in Recognition Decision?	Other Information on Recognition
Rwanda (cont.)	1969	Yes	Yes			Yes	No	litical consideration; uses diplomatic relations in its political responses.
Senegal	1969	Yes				Yes		
Sierra Leone	1969	No				Yes		No set policy; tries to avoid question. Goes along with majority of African states.
Somalia	1969	No				Yes, based on budgetary factors.	Yes	Not well-defined; based on self-interest.
Republic of South Africa	1969	No	Yes			Yes		Recognition should be positive, overt act.

Country	Year						Notes
	1975	No	No	Yes	Yes	Yes	Not overt act.
Sudan	1969	No	Yes	No	Yes	Yes	Ad hoc; no clear policy.
Tanzania	1969	No	Yes	Yes	Yes, based on budgetary factors.	Yes	Political interests & moral factors important; no clear policy; tradition criteria.
Togo	1969	Yes, generally because of numerous coups.	No	Yes	No	No	No clear policy; exception to Estrada based on policy considerations.
Tunisia	1969	Yes, but will withhold recognition.		Yes	No, diplomatic relations possible only after recognition.	Yes	See note 21.
Uganda	1969	Yes			No		Might deviate in special case; mainly concerned with Africa.
Upper Volta	1969	Yes			No		No set policy; depends on circumstances.

Appendix A (continued)

State	Year	Does State Follow Estrada Doctrine?	Is Effective Control a Factor in Grant of Recognition?	Is Willingness to Honor International Obligations a Factor in Grant of Recognition?	Is Consent of the People a Factor in Grant of Recognition?	Is Distinction Made between Recognition and Diplomatic Relations?	Are Political Factors Important in Recognition Decision?	Other Information on Recognition
Zambia	1969	No	Yes, important.			No	Yes	Ad hoc; moral & political considerations weighed in light of national interest.
NEAR EAST AND SOUTH ASIA								
Afghanistan	1969	No	Yes			Yes	Yes	Pragmatic; based on political factors.
Ceylon	1969	Never considered the question.						
Cyprus	1969	No				No	Yes, most important.	Follows traditional policy. Legal justifications devised after policy decision.

Country	Year							Description
Iran	1969	No					Yes	Traditional policy; all facts of each case considered.
	1975	No	Yes	Yes	Yes	Yes		Historical, social, economic, political relations reviewed; self-interest important.
Israel	1969	No	No					No set policy; evaluate each on its own merit..
Jordan	1969	No			Yes	Yes	Yes	Ad hoc; more political than legal; policy of other Arab states important.
Kuwait	1969	Yes, with exceptions. For political reasons.	Yes, important except when very strong political factors.		Yes	Yes	Yes	Diplomatic relations based on political considerations.
Lebanon	1969	No	Yes	Yes	Yes	Yes	Yes	Final decision based on national interest.

Appendix A (continued)

State	Year	Does State Follow Estrada Doctrine?	Is Effective Control a Factor in Grant of Recognition?	Is Willingness to Honor International Obligations a Factor in Grant of Recognition?	Is Consent of the People a Factor in Grant of Recognition?	Is Distinction Made between Recognition and Diplomatic Relations?	Are Political Factors Important in Recognition Decision?	Other Information on Recognition
Nepal	1969	Yes, but no fixed policy.				Yes	Yes	National interest important; ad hoc.
Pakistan	1969	No	Yes	Yes		Yes	Yes	If gov't. in firm control, Pakistan will recognize if in national interest.
Saudi Arabia	1969	Recognize state, not government, usually.				Yes	Yes	No detailed criteria; political factors important, ad hoc.
Southern Yemen	1969	No				Not yet decided.	Yes, most important.	No set policy.
Turkey	1969	Yes				No		Question of criteria does not arise.

Country	Year							Remarks
United Arab Republic	1969	No					Yes	Ad hoc; no official policy.
Australia	1969	No, but often extends recognition almost automatically.	Yes	Yes	No practical distinction.		No	Is gov't in power and will it stay in power? If so Australia will grant recog.
	1975	No	Yes	Yes	See note 22.	See note 22.	No	See note 22.
Republic of China	1969	Yes	Yes		No		Yes	See note 23.
Indonesia	1969	Yes, generally.	Yes		No		No	
	1975	Yes, generally.	Yes		No		Yes	
Japan	1969	No, but has de-emphasized recognition.			Yes	Yes	Yes	Looks to actions of neighboring states & U.S.; ad hoc; political decision.

Appendix A (continued)

State	Year	Does State Follow Estrada Doctrine?	Is Effective Control a Factor in Grant of Recognition?	Is Willingness to Honor International Obligations a Factor in Grant of Recognition?	Is Consent of the People a Factor in Grant of Recognition?	Is Distinction Made between Recognition and Diplomatic Relations?	Are Political Factors Important in Recognition Decision?	Other Information on Recognition
Japan (cont.)	1975	No	Yes	Yes		Yes	Yes	
Laos	1969	Yes, with some exceptions.				Yes	Yes	Laos's neutrality key political factor.
South Korea	1969	No	Yes	Yes	Yes	Yes	Yes, important.	Political decision, N. Korea a factor, no fixed policy.
Malaysia	1969	No	Yes		Yes	Not usually.	Yes	Legal criteria prerequisite, then political decision; no set criteria.
New Zealand	1969	No	Yes	No				Pragmatic; usually goes along with British view; no set criteria.
	1975	No	Yes	No	See note 24.	See note 24.	See note 24.	See note 24.

Country	Year						Notes
Philippines	1969	No	Yes			Yes	Traditional policy; ad hoc.
	1975	No. See note 25.	Yes	Yes	Yes	Yes	See note 25.
Singapore	1969	No	Yes		Yes—budgetary reasons.	Yes	Deemphasizes recognition decision.
South Vietnam	1969	No	Yes		Yes—based on budget.	Yes	Traditional policy; political factors decisive.

EUROPE

Country	Year						Notes
Austria	1969	No	Yes				Ad hoc; pragmatic.
	1975	In effect; see note 26.	No				
Belgium	1969	Yes, in practice; some exceptions, if asked.					Diplomatic relations determined in effective control & popular assent; pragmatic based on national interest.

Appendix A (continued)

State	Year	Does State Follow Estrada Doctrine?	Is Effective Control a Factor in Grant of Recognition?	Is Willingness to Honor International Obligations a Factor in Grant of Recognition?	Is Consent of the People a Factor in Grant of Recognition?	Is Distinction Made between Recognition and Diplomatic Relations?	Are Political Factors Important in Recognition Decision?	Other Information on Recognition
Belgium (cont.)	1975	Yes, in practice.						General practice to recognize states, not gov't., pragmatic.
Bulgaria	1969	No					Yes, important.	Often attempts to avoid issue; U.S.S.R. action important, flexible.
Canada	1969	No	Yes	Yes	Yes	Yes—based on budget.		Traditionally, act basically legal. Still area for political factors.
	1975	No	Yes	Yes	Yes		Yes	See note 27.
								U.S.S.R. important; often maintains diplomatic relations

					Yes, some-times.	Yes	without com-menting on recognition.
Czechoslovakia	1969	No					
Denmark	1969	No, not familiar with doctrine.	Yes		Yes—financial reasons.		Traditional policy.
Denmark	1975	No, not familiar with doctrine.	Yes	No	Yes—budgetary reasons.	No	Traditional policy.
Finland	1969	Yes			No		
Finland	1975	In effect; see note 28.	Yes		See note 28.	No	No
France	1969	Yes	Yes		Yes	No	Political factors can enter.
West Germany	1969	Yes, some exceptions.			Yes		For dipl. rel., is gov. in power & is it in best interest of democracy.
West Germany	1975	See note 29.		Yes	Yes		See note 29.
Great Britain	1969	No	Yes	Yes	Obedience instead of consent.		
Great Britain	1975	No	Yes			No	See note 30.

Appendix A (continued)

State	Year	Does State Follow Estrada Doctrine?	Is Effective Control a Factor in Grant of Recognition?	Is Willingness to Honor International Obligations a Factor in Grant of Recognition?	Is Consent of the People a Factor in Grant of Recognition?	Is Distinction Made between Recognition and Diplomatic Relations?	Are Political Factors Important in Recognition Decision?	Other Information on Recognition
Greece	1969	No	Yes			Yes		Acts according to principles of int'l. law.
Iceland	1969	No					Yes	Ad hoc; nat'l. interest imp.; views of Nordic states imp.
	1975	No					Yes	Flexible, ad hoc not important issue.
Ireland	1969	Normally, recognizes states and not governments.	Yes	Yes		Yes		No question of recog. until question of dipl. rel.
		Used some-						Acts of interested states & allies imp.; legal position often justifica-

Italy	1969	time, but not controlling.	Yes	Yes	Not usually.	Yes	tion for policy position.
	1975	See note 31.				Yes	Basically, political decision.
Netherlands	1969	No	Yes	Yes	No	Yes	
	1975	See note 32.					
Norway	1969	No	Yes, important.		Yes, although maintenance of relations may imply recognition.		
Poland	1969	No	Yes, important.	Yes		No	If gov't. is in effective control, will recognize.
Portugal	1969	Generally recognizes states and not governments.			Emphasis on maintaining relations, recognition a formality.		Flexible.
Rumania	1969	No	Yes	Yes	Yes	Yes, important.	
Spain	1969	No				Yes	Ad hoc.
Sweden							Actions of neighboring

Appendix A (continued)

State	Year	Does State Follow Estrada Doctrine?	Is Effective Control a Factor in Grant of Recognition?	Is Willingness to Honor International Obligations a Factor in Grant of Recognition?	Is Consent of the People a Factor in Grant of Recognition?	Is Distinction Made between Recognition and Diplomatic Relations?	Are Political Factors Important in Recognition Decision?	Other Information on Recognition
Sweden (cont.)	1969	No				Yes		states & large powers important.
	1975	No	Yes	No, generally.	No	Yes	No	Actions of neighboring states & large powers important.
Switzerland	1975	Pertains to specific situations.	Yes	No	No	No		See note 33.
U.S.S.R.	1969	No					Yes	Pragmatic; self-interest guiding factor.
Yugoslavia	1969	No	Yes			Yes	Yes, important.	Political factor still most important.
	1975	No	Yes			Yes	Yes, important.	Political factor still most important.

Notes to Appendix A

[1] This survey is based on a 1969 circular telegram from the Department of State to all American embassies and on a 1975 letter from the author to all states that were contacted in the 1969 survey. The table itself supplies most of the information obtained in the two surveys. However, several states, in addition to answering particular questions on their recognition policy, commented on their policy; this material is footnoted in the column titled "other information on recognition." The sources of the information in these notes are responses to the circular telegram unless otherwise noted.

[2] Recognition takes the form of entry into, continuation of, or resumption of diplomatic relations. Respect for human rights is a criterion. Argentina is wary of withholding recognition because of the possibility of intervention charge.

[3] Bolivia recognizes new governments only after reasonable delay and consultations with other nations, as under Resolution XXVI.

[4] Brazil does not have an established list of criteria; however, criteria include respect for human rights, stability, administrative continuity; there is no rigid doctrine—changes of government are handled on a case-by-case basis; Brazil also allows an adequate waiting period.

[5] Chile gives consideration to vicinity, traditional friendship, and other background on a case-by-case basis. However, the fact that sustaining diplomatic relations is above all a sovereign act must be borne in mind. Letter from Embassy of Chile to author, November 3, 1975.

[6] Costa Rica until 1966 followed the Betancourt Doctrine. It now considers respect for human rights an important factor.

[7] Ecuador usually follows the traditional formula. It also consults with other OAS members prior to the recognition of de facto government, recommended in Resolution XXVI. Letter from Embassy of Ecuador to author, October 22, 1975.

[8] El Salvador generally follows Resolution XXVI criteria; its timing is influenced by domestic considerations. Basically, El Salvador follows traditional policy.

[9] Guatemala believes that a change of government is an internal affair. There has been a recent change in policy.

[10] Haiti follows a traditional policy; it is careful not to take the lead, and will wait until majority position is apparent.

[11] Jamaica follows the "British" practice. It waits a reasonable period of time to determine effective control. It makes no announcement unless requested.

[12] Nicaragua's recognition policy is based on Resolution XXVI and the Resolution on the Right of Legation, adopted by the 1945 Bogota Conference.

[13] Uruguay followed a traditional policy until 1967 and made a formal decree of recognition. Now Uruguay just acknowledges with a note.

[14] Venezuela until 1964 followed the Betancourt Doctrine; now it follows a traditional pragmatic policy with no automatic formula.

[15] For Algeria, the most important factor in recognition is political. Algeria follows a flexible and pragmatic policy. It tries to finesse the issue of whether a new act of recognition is involved.

[16] Botswana follows a traditional policy. The policy is a combination of practical necessity and ideological and political sympathy.

[17] The foreign policy of Burundi (Benin) is based on the principle of nonalignment, the noninterference in the internal affairs of other countries, and on international cooperation with all nations regardless of their social regime with the exceptions of the apartheid and racial discrimination policies of South Africa and Rhodesia. Letter from Embassy of Burundi to author, October 20, 1975.

18 Cameroon has no procedure for recognizing new governments or states with which diplomatic relations are maintained.

19 Central African Republic (Empire) has little more than a pragmatic policy with virtually no philosophic base. Traditional criteria are used. The president is strongly anti-Communist and this affects decisions.

20 The Ivory Coast recognizes only states; therefore the question of criteria for recognition of new governments does not arise. The Ivory Coast will use national interest and moral consideration to decide on diplomatic relations.

21 Tunisia's criteria for recognizing governments are popular support, constitution in accord with international law, and political factors. Also it considers other states' views.

22 Australia considers the control of the new government, the consent of the people, and the willingness of the new government to have international obligations in its decision to extend recognition. It does not consider political factors. In its response to the 1975 letter from the author, the Department of Foreign Affairs also noted:

> *Distinction between Recognition and Diplomatic Relations. Note:* The response here depends on the meaning of "diplomatic relations." If it means exchange of diplomatic representatives, then there is a distinction because such an exchange need not flow from recognition. If, however, diplomatic relations is intended to be broader, so as to mean the normalization of diplomatic relations and international intercourse, then that is a direct consequence of recognition.
>
> *Political Factors.* The Australian government pursues a policy of universality in its recognition decisions. Accordingly, recognition of governments should flow from the appraisal of traditional criteria, and should not be determined by arbitrary political factors.
>
> *Other Factors.* The exercise of effective control and a reasonable prospect of permanence.

Letter to author from Australian Embassy, December 1, 1975.

23 The Republic of China will recognize practically any government which does not recognize the People's Republic of China and which will recognize the Republic of China.

24 "New Zealand applies this criterion [consent of the people] in deciding whether governments should be recognized on the basis that the competence of a political body to make promises on behalf of a community, and generally to represent that community, is directly related to its apparent ability to secure fulfillment of its promises.

"Strictly as formulated, a 'willingness' to observe international commitments is not a pre-condition for recognition, although such willingness is naturally taken into account as a 'political factor' (see below).

"Formulated as an 'ability' rather than as a 'willingness' to observe such commitments, however, the criterion is considered a pre-requisite: an entity, to be recognized as a state, must be independent and thus have the capacity to enter into international commitments and to carry them out. Equally, where the recognition of governments is concerned, the ability to observe international commitments is required, though here of course such ability is merely an aspect of effectiveness of control.

"In the sense that a government must succeed through constitutional legitimacy or as a result of the democratic expression of the wishes of the people it governs, New Zealand does not insist on this as a pre-requisite to recognition, although such factors may be important. In the sense of governmental stability, however, the criterion is important: the government concerned must have a reasonable prospect of permanency and the support of political or popular groups representing a majority in the political system. Once again this could be considered an aspect of effectiveness of control.

178

"New Zealand distinguishes between the two in the sense that recognition of a new government does not necessarily automatically entail the initiating of an exchange of diplomatic representatives. In some cases, however, where New Zealand diplomatic representatives remain in a country after an unconstitutional change of government and deal with the new government authorities as if diplomatic relations continued, then that presence may be intended as tantamount to continued recognition. In such cases New Zealand has, in conformity with modern practice, preferred to evidence by conduct (rather than by a formal declaration of recognition) its acceptance of the competence of a new government to act for a recognized state.

"The general legal criteria of recognition are used by the New Zealand government in assessing whether a particular entity is *capable* of being regarded as a state or a government. (Shortly stated, these criteria are, of course, that an entity is in law generally deemed to be a state if it has a territory, a population, a government independent of other governments and a measure of stability. Again, an entity is generally understood to be the government of a state if it is in effective control of the state, is independent and enjoys a measure of stability.) You will, of course, be aware that there has been some controversy as to whether or not there is a legal duty to recognize a state or a government when criteria such as those mentioned above are fulfilled. The New Zealand government does not share the view that any such legal duty arises in these circumstances, and regards the decision of whether or not to grant recognition as one of political policy. Both a willingness to observe international obligations and the constitutionality of any change of government may be important factors influencing the policy decision on whether or not to recognize.

"Account is taken, where change of government occurs extra constitutionally, of the level of continuity with the previous government, the directions in which the new government is moving and whether extra constitutional change is in fact the norm in the country concerned."

Letter from Embassy of New Zealand to author, March 1, 1976.

[25] The government of the Philippines explained its regular policy in 1975 in the following manner: "The Philippines does not accord diplomatic recognition ipso facto to foreign governments which have come to power through extra-legal or extra constitutional means." Of the Estrada Doctrine, Salonga's Public International Law has this to say: "In 1930, the Mexican Foreign Minister Estrada, enunciated a doctrine (popularly called Estrada doctrine) that where a new government is established in another country by revolutionary means, Mexico would continue diplomatic relations, so far as possible, with the new government without regard to the legitimacy.

"The underlying idea is that one State has no right to pass judgment on the legitimacy of a new government as this would involve an inquiry into the internal affairs of another state. This seems to be erroneous, since the inquiry is not into the legitimacy of the Government but into its representative character." (Salonga & Yap, *Public International Law*, 4th ed., Ch. 5, p. 105.)

"The Philippines recognizes the principle of effective control as a criterion in the grant of diplomatic recognition to foreign governments. This is in accordance with generally accepted principles of international law.

"Before recognition is accorded to foreign governments which have come to power through extra constitutional means or otherwise, they must possess certain minimal requisites; one of which is the desire and capacity to honour and discharge international obligations.

"The Philippines subscribes to the generally recognized principles of international law. Aruego notes that certain standards for diplomatic recognition have been worked out in the course of the years in the practice of states. These have been stability and willingness and ability of the new government to meet its international obligations. (Jose M. Aruego, *International Law Reviewer*, 1957, Ch. 6, p. 43.)

179

"Inasmuch as the Philippines follows the principle of effectiveness which states that the new government, to be entitled to recognition, ought to be supported by the will of the nation, substantially declared.

"The Philippine position is that we may recognize a State and the government in control of that state, but it does not necessarily follow that we open diplomatic relations with it. We recognize the government of the USSR but have no diplomatic relations with it as yet. In the case of the new Cambodian government, which is an example of a government which has come into power in a State which we already recognize, we gave recognition to the new Government but still do not have diplomatic relations with it."

Letter from Embassy of the Philippines to author, November 5, 1975.

26 It remains the policy of the Republic of Austria to maintain that a change of government does not affect the identity of a state as a subject of international law. The relations among states are confined to being relations among subjects of international law. According to the Austrian point of view, the question by whom or by which organs these relations are carried out is a matter to be determined by the laws and by the factual situation of the other state. Since Austria does not expressly recognize foreign governments there is no need to consider the effectiveness of governments. Letter from Embassy of Austria to author, February 20, 1976.

27 "The recognition of governments involves a consideration as to whether an authority claiming to be the government of a state is able to exercise effective control with a reasonable prospect of permanency in the area which it claims to govern; the support it enjoys of the population and its expressed willingness to fulfill its international obligations may also be taken into account. While the act of recognition is essentially legal in nature, the relevancy of political factors is recognized in modern international practice; each situation is therefore considered on its own merit. Most of the time, however, when an orderly change of government, or type of government occurs in a territorial entity recognized by Canada as a state, the question of recognition does not arise. In such cases, the recognition already granted to a previous government continues to apply to its successors."

Canadian Yearbook of International Law, vol. 10 (1972), quoting letter of July 23, 1971 from Mitchell Sharp, secretary of state for external affairs. Canada was placed in the European section of the appendix because its interests and approach more closely parallel European practice then Latin American.

28 "It is the policy of Finland to recognize States rather than governments. Finland considers recognition of a State as declaratory only.

"Study of the expose on the Estrada Doctrine in Whiteman's *Digest of International Law* Vol. 2 & 4 p. 88 et seq. indicates that the doctrine seems to have evolved and to have been applied with the States of the Western Hemisphere in view and to have been limited expressly to the question of de facto recognition of governments. Thus, it is not adequate to combine the Finnish policy in this respect with the Estrada Doctrine.

"Finland stipulates as prerequisites for recognition of States the criteria postulated for statehood in international law, namely: the existence of a defined territory, population, and effective government.

"Referring to the Finnish policy of recognizing only States, Finland does not establish diplomatic relations with governments. Recognition of a State does not presuppose the establishment of diplomatic relations. As an example of Finnish recognition policy we cite Finnish recognition of the two German States. Both were recognized by Finland on 19 November 1972 and diplomatic relations were established with both States on 7 January 1973."

Letter from Embassy of Finland to author, February 10, 1976.

29 "The Federal Government decides on a case by case basis whether the condi-

tions are fulfilled that a new government may be regarded under international law as speaker of its country.

"Even if these conditions are fulfilled under international law and political aspects, there will not be a formal declaration of recognition but merely a continuation of the diplomatic relations to the other State with the new government which is implicitly a recognition of the new government.

"In special exceptional cases, however, it could be possible that the Federal Government will not rest satisfied with such an implicit recognition.

"There is a difference in the definition of a recognition of a new government and the establishment of diplomatic relations with a government as recognition is an unilateral act, and the establishment of diplomatic relations a bilateral act.

"On the other hand, on the occasion of an implicit recognition by continuing the diplomatic relations, both facts are inseparably linked with each other."
Letter from West German Embassy to author, December 17, 1975.

30 "The United Kingdom Government's position is that a regime claiming to be the Government of State is entitled to recognition as such if it may fairly be held to enjoy, with a reasonable prospect of permanency, the obedience of the mass of the population and the effective control of much the greater part of the national territory.

"Recognition is the acknowledgment of an existing factual situation and does not imply any moral judgment or approval of the regime in question."
Letter to author from British Embassy, November 24, 1975.

31 "It has to be noted anyhow, that diplomatic recognition is, for Italy as for other European states, less an instrument of policy than it is for the United States.

"In recent cases, as for example in our relations with Cambodia and Chile, we have avoided taking an explicit position on the problem of recognition, which we consider pertaining to the area of relations between States themselves; we have instead however 'suspended' or 'reduced' diplomatic relations between Governments.

"I noticed that you have left blank the question concerning the *consent* of the people of the State in which extra-constitutional change occurred. It is in fact, a delicate and controversial question. I would place it rather under *other factors*, as an element whose presence or absence might discourage or encourage recognition in combination with other political considerations.

"The problem, as I see it, is further complicated by the need of assessing the means of determining the consent itself; by elections, by protracted guerrilla warfare, by other significant actions of a relevant part of the population."
Letter from Embassy of Italy to author, October 14, 1975.

32 "The Ministry now informs me that it seems hardly possible to describe the Netherlands policy with regard to recognition of new governments using the 'yes-no' format contained in your list. It would seem that your conclusions with regard to said practice do not take sufficiently into account the weight carried by the listed criteria in different concrete cases. Furthermore, it should be pointed out that in considering recognition or continuing of any one form of diplomatic relations with a new government, the question whether this government respects fundamental human rights plays an important role."
Letter from Embassy of the Netherlands to author, November 3, 1975.

33 Switzerland explained its recognition policy in 1975 in the following manner:
Estrada Doctrine: The Estrada Doctrine seems to pertain to specific situations. It may however be said that this Doctrine was applied by Switzerland in the case of the Spanish Civil War. Angola might be considered another example of that Doctrine.
Effective Control: Yes.
International Obligations: No—international obligations are neither abso-

lute nor sufficiently precise to serve as references in the grant of recognition. In that field, reference to a specific obligation might prove a necessity (as the Stimson Doctrine refers to the Pact of Paris of August 27, 1928).

Consent: No.

Distinction between Recognition and Diplomatic Relations: Switzerland recognizes States, not governments. (Example: China in 1949.)

Political Factors—Importance in Recognition Decisions: See above statement.

Other Factors: To be recognized, a State should conform to the definition prevailing in international law: an entity represented by a body of people politically organized under a sovereign government within a territory having definite boundaries.

Summary of letter from Embassy of Switzerland to author, undated.

Table B-1

SPECIFIC CRITERIA FOR U.S. RESPONSE TO EXTRACONSTITUTIONAL CHANGES OF GOVERNMENT, 1960–1969

Specific Criterion	Number of Instances Cited
1. Effective control of government machinery	5
2. Public acquiescence	0
3. Intent to honor international obligations and commitments	17
4. Evidence of foreign intervention	1
5. Political orientation of the government and people	4
6. Intent to hold election and/or observe democratic principles	13
7. Intent to strengthen ties with United States	1
8. Intent to respect human rights	2
9. Intent to comply with constitution	6
10. Intent to improve social and economic conditions	3
11. Election details	5
12. Stress inter-American system	1
13. Foreign policy orientation, such as maintaining friendly relations with democratic governments or neighbors	2
14. Intent to maintain cordial relations with the United States	5

Source: Material drawn from Joan K. Wadlow, "Recent U.S. Recognition Policy toward Coups d'Etat," appendix (unpublished manuscript on file with author).

Table B-2

CRITERIA CITED BY THE UNITED STATES IN RECOGNIZING GOVERNMENTS ESTABLISHED BY COUP d'ETAT DURING THE 1960s

Country	Date of Overthrow	Summary of Response	Statement in State Department Bulletin	Specific Criteria[a]
El Salvador	10/26/60	Recognition extended on 12/3/60	X	3,6,8,9
El Salvador	1/25/61	Recognition extended on 2/15/61	X	1,3,6,10,13
South Korea	5/16/61	Question did not arise		
Syria	3/2/62	Recognition extended 3/7/62	X	14
Argentina	3/29/62	Relations continued without interruption: statement issued 4/18/62	X	
Peru	7/18/62	Relations suspended: recognition extended 8/17/62	X	1,3,6,9,11,12
Yemen	9/27/62	Relations suspended: recognition extended 12/19/62	X	3,4,10,11,13
Togo	1/13/63	Relations suspended: recognition extended 6/6/63	X	3,5,6
Iraq	2/8/63	Recognition extended 2/11/63	X	3,14
Syria	3/8/63	Recognition extended 3/12/63	X	3,14
Guatemala	3/30/63	Recognition extended 4/17/63	X	1,3,6
Equador	7/11/63	Recognition extended 7/31/63	X	6,9
Dominican Republic	7/25/63	Normal relations ended pending recognition 12/14/63	X	3,5,6,11
Honduras	10/3/63	Same as above	X	3,5,6,11
Dahomey	10/28/63	Recognition extended 1/31/64	X	3,6,11
South Vietnam	11/1/63	Relations continued: statement issued 11/8/63	X	

Country	Date	Status	Recognition	Notes
Zanzibar	1/12/64	Recognition extended 2/24/64		
South Vietnam	1/30/64	Question did not arise: statement issued 2/1/64	X	3
Brazil	4/1/64	Question did not arise	X	
Sudan	10/26/64	Question did not arise	X	
Bolivia	11/6/64	Relations suspended: recognition statement issued 12/8/64	X	1,3,6,9
Dominican Republic	4/24/65	Recognition statement issued 9/4/65	X	3,5,6,10
South Vietnam	6/11/65	Question did not arise		
Algeria	6/19/65	Relations not broken according to press report 7/19/65		
Congo	11/25/65	Relations continued according to press report 12/8/65		
Dahomey	12/22/65	No interruption in relations according to announcement 1/29/66		
Central African Republic (Empire)	1/1/66	Question did not arise: announcement authorized 2/10/66		
Upper Volta	1/4/66	Question did not arise: announcement authorized 2/10/66		
Nigeria	1/15/66	No interruption in relations according to announcement 1/29/66		
Syria	2/23/66	Question did not arise		
Ghana	2/24/66	Recognition extended 3/4/66	X	
Equador	3/31/66	Relations continued without interruption: statement issued 4/12/66	X	
Argentina	6/28/66	Relations suspended: recognition extended 7/15/66	X	14
Burundi	7/11/66	Question did not arise		
Nigeria	7/29/66	Question did not arise		
Burundi	11/29/66	Question did not arise		
Sierra Leone	3/22/67	Question did not arise		

Table B-2 (continued)

Country	Date of Overthrow	Summary of Response	Statement in State Department Bulletin	Specific Criteria[a]
Greece	4/27/67	Top level formal contact ended in December after king's departure; announcement made 1/23/68 that recognition question did not arise.		
Dahomey	12/17/67	Question did not arise		
Sierra Leone	4/18/68	Question did not arise		
Congo-Brazzaville	9/3/68	Question did not arise		
Peru	10/3/68	Relations suspended: recognition extended 10/25/68	X	3,6,9
Panama	10/11/68	Relations suspended: recognition extended 11/13/68	X	3,6,8,9
Mali	11/19/68	Question did not arise		
Sudan	5/25/69	U.S. did not have diplomatic relations		
Southern Yemen	6/23/69	Question did not arise		
Libya	9/1/69	Relations continued: announcement made 9/6/69		1,3,14
Bolivia	9/26/69	Relations continued: statement issued 10/10/69	X	7
Somalia	10/21/69	Question did not arise		
Dahomey	12/10/69	Question did not arise		

a Criteria listed in Table B-1.
Source: Material drawn from Joan K. Wadlow, "Recent U.S. Recognition Policy toward Coups d'Etat," Appendix (unpublished manuscript on file with author).

Table B-3

RECOGNITION OF EXTRACONSTITUTIONAL CHANGES IN
GOVERNMENTS UNDER PRESIDENT KENNEDY

Nation	Coup Date	Date of Recognition	Time Lapse (days)	Criteria Cited	Nations Consulted
Eastern Hemisphere					
Syria	9/28/61	10/10/61	8	Fulfill international obligations	UAR, UK
Syria	3/8/63	3/12/63	5	same	UK
Burma	3/2/62	3/7/62	5	same	
Yemen	9/27/62	12/19/62	84	same	UK
Iraq	2/8/63	2/10/63	3	same	UK
Togo	1/13/63	6/6/63	144	same	Followed lead of neighboring states
S. Vietnam	11/2/63	11/8/63	6	same	
Western Hemisphere					
El Salvador	1/25/61	2/15/61	21	Democratic elections, international obligations	OAS nations
Argentina	3/29/62	4/18/62[a]	20	same	same
Peru	7/18/62	3/17/62	30	same	same
Guatemala	3/31/63	4/17/63	19	same	same
Ecuador	7/11/63	7/31/63	20	same	same
Dominican Republic	9/25/63	12/14/63	79	same	same
Honduras	12/3/63	12/14/63	11	same	same

[a] Resumed relations.

Source: Material drawn from Charles L. Cochran, "The Recognition of States and Governments by President John F. Kennedy" (Ph.D. diss., Tufts University, 1969), Appendix, p. 8.

BIBILOGRAPHY

Books

Cole, Taylor. *The Recognition Policy of the United States since 1901.*
Baton Rouge: Louisiana State University, 1928.

Goebel, Julius, Jr. *The Recognition Policy of the United States.* New
York: Columbia University, 1915.

Hackworth, Green. *Digest of International Law,* vol. 1. Washington,
D.C.: Department of State, 1940.

Jaffe, Louis L. *Judicial Aspects of Foreign Relations.* Cambridge, Mass.:
Harvard University Press, 1933.

Jessup, Philip C. *A Modern Law of Nations.* New York: The Macmillan Co., 1948.

Lauterpacht, Hersh. *Recognition in International Law.* Cambridge,
England: University Press, 1947.

Lieuwen, Edwin. *Generals vs. Presidents—Neomilitarism in Latin
America.* New York: Praeger, 1964.

McMahon, John L. *Recent Changes in the Recognition Policy of the
United States.* Washington, D.C.: Catholic University, 1933.

Moore, John Basset. *A Digest of International Law,* vol. 1. Washington, D.C.: Government Printing Office, 1906.

Neumann, William. *Recognition of Governments in the Americas.*
Washington, D.C.: Foundation for Foreign Affairs, 1947.

Whiteman, M. *Digest of International Law,* vol. 2. Washington, D.C.:
Department of State, 1963.

Dissertation

Cochran, Charles L., "The Recognition of States and Governments
by President John F. Kennedy: An Analysis." Ph.D. diss., Tufts
University, 1969.

Articles

Brown, P. "The Legal Effects of Recognition." *American Journal of International Law* 44: 617.

Buell, R. "The United States and Central American Stability." *Foreign Policy Reports* 7: 161.

————. "The United States and Central American Revolutions." *Foreign Policy Reports* 7: 187.

Dozier, D. "Recognition in Inter-American Relations." *Journal of Inter-American Studies* 8: 335.

Fenwick, C. "The Recognition of New Governments Instituted by Force." *American Journal of International Law* 38: 448.

————. "The Recognition of *De Facto* Governments: Is There a Basis for Inter-American Collective Action?" *American Journal of International Law* 58: 109.

Lafore, L. "The Problem of Diplomatic Recognition." *Current History* 30: 158.

Lauterpacht, H. "Recognition of Governments: I." *Columbia Law Review* 45: 815.

————. "Recognition of Governments: II." *Columbia Law Review* 46: 37.

Maher, Theodore. "The Kennedy and Johnson Responses to Latin American Coups d'Etat." *World Affairs* 131: 184.

Needler, Martin. "United States Recognition Policy and the Peruvian Case." *Inter-American Economic Affairs* 16: 61.

Wadlow, J. "Recent U.S. Recognition Policy toward Coups d'Etat." Unpublished.

Government Publications

Public Papers of the Presidents of the United States: John F. Kennedy. "Press Conference of February 10, 1961." Washington, D.C., 1962, p. 92.

United States Congress, Senate, Committee on Foreign Relations. *Hearings on Sen. Res. 205,* 91st Cong., 1st sess. (June 17, 1969), Washington, D.C.

U.S. Department of State. *Developments in U.S. Relations with Brazil, 1824–Present,* 71 Dept. of State Bulletin 345 (September 2, 1974).

U.S. Department of State. *Developments in U.S. Relations with Uruguay, 1828—Present,* 70 Dept. of State Bulletin 613 (June 3, 1974).

U.S. Department of State. *Diplomatic Correspondence.* vol. 2 (1868), p. 864.

U.S. Department of State. *The Problem of Recognition in Amerian Foreign Policy,* Research Project 174, Division of Historical Policy Research, August 1950.

U.S. Department of State. *U.S. Policy toward Latin America: Recognition and Non-Recognition of Governments and Interruptions in Diplomatic Relations, 1933-1974.* Bureau of Public Affairs, Historical Office, June 1975.